MARK LAWRENSON
THE AUTOBIOGRAPHY

MARK LAWRENSON
THE AUTOBIOGRAPHY

Mark Lawrenson with Mike Ellis

Macdonald
Queen Anne Press

A QUEEN ANNE PRESS BOOK

© *Queen Anne Press* 1988

A Pergamon Press plc company
Designed by: Dave Crook
Jacket photographs – Front: Sporting Pictures (UK) Ltd
Back: Colorsport

First published in Great Britain in 1988 by
Queen Anne Press, a division of
Macdonald & Co (Publishers) Ltd
3rd Floor
Greater London House
Hampstead Road
London
NW1 7QX

The publishers would like to thank the following for their permission to
use copyright material/photographs:
Allsport/Dave Cannon: pp 6b, 9, 11t, 12, 16; Associated Sports
Photography: p 3; Colorsport: pp 4t, 8; Daily Mirror: p 5; Mark
Lawrenson: pp 1t & b, 7; Press Association Ltd: pp 2t & b (Preston North
End F.C.); Bob Thomas: pp 4b, 6t, 10, 11b, 13, 14, 15.

British Library Cataloguing in Publication Data

Lawrenson, Mark
  Mark Lawrenson autobiography.
  1. Lawrenson, Mark   2. Soccer players—
  Ireland—autobiography
  I. Title
  796.334'092'4   GV942.7.L37

  ISBN 0-356-15285-5

Typeset by Butler & Tanner Ltd
Printed and bound in Great Britain by
Hazell Watson & Viney Limited
Member of the BPCC Group
Aylesbury, Bucks

CONTENTS

This book is dedicated to Vanessa, my family and the friends who have encouraged me throughout my career

FOREWORD BY BOB PAISLEY

Mark Lawrenson was Liverpool's record buy at the time but even at £900,000 I rated him a steal and his contribution to Liverpool's cause since he arrived merely confirms that view. I am convinced it was his injury last season which cost Liverpool the chance of a major prize. We had already lost other senior players but Mark's ability to play in a variety of roles is invaluable to the team. Wherever he is performing he makes an impact and as a senior professional he leads by example. Everything he does is so clean cut that I would want him dealing with a one-to-one situation in the penalty box ahead of any other defender. He has been a model professional for Liverpool and will be for some time to come.

We had been keeping tabs on Mark's progress at Brighton, but the match which clinched it in our minds was his performance against Kenny Dalglish when the two met for the first time. There are few players around today who can perform at the highest level in so many different roles, particularly when first and foremost they are recognised as outstanding central defenders. When I describe him as somebody who just gets on with the job without any fuss, I am paying him the biggest of compliments.

Bob Paisley

MY FOOTBALL HERITAGE

I was raised in a football-mad environment so perhaps it's inevitable that I followed in my father's footsteps and became a professional. Home was Preston where my dad Tommy played for North End during the Tom Finney era in the '50s. As he was also a winger he didn't get many first team opportunities because that was the great man's favourite position too. My father spent 12 years as a pro moving on to Southport in the old Third Division North and ending with a spell of non-League football at Morecambe. My parents split up when I was 12 and my mother Theresa married Tom Gore who had played the game as a part-time professional before becoming a director at Preston. One way and another, therefore, soccer made an early impression on me although it was my mum who was the guiding light and always managed to watch me play when I was a schoolboy. She was my biggest fan right from the start and I have never forgotten that.

At school I was a centre forward and I must have shown some promise because when I was eight I was playing for the Under-11 team and by the time I was 10 I had been selected for the Preston Schools District team and remember scoring twice in my first game for them. I had an immediate incentive to pass my 11-plus because I was desperate to go to the Preston Catholic College which was a very sports-orientated school. Just imagine, 14 football pitches – that sounded like paradise for a lad who had already caught the bug and was dreaming of playing for Manchester United. They were *the* team in those days; all the kids idolised George Best, Denis Law and Bobby Charlton. Little did I know that one day the great Bobby himself would ask me to sign professional for Preston. Liverpool was just another team to me then and hardly rated a thought in the mind of an eager young boy who could think only of Old Trafford and that wonderful side they had at the time.

In later years there was a possibility of my signing for United when I decided to leave Brighton, and Ron Atkinson was certainly interested, but another team in red were the top outfit in the country by then and I took all of 20 minutes to sign for them when they made their offer. Liverpool was a million miles away from my thoughts when I started at the Catholic College. The Jesuit priests were all sports crazy and their enthusiasm certainly got through to me; so did the advice and guidance of the sports master Peter Singleton. Ask any player fortunate enough to have made it to the top and I'm sure they can all rattle off the name of their sports master because at that age you are very impressionable, and if the man in charge is good at his job you never forget the help and encouragement which was available at that stage.

Soccer was not the only sport I was hooked on, however. Cricket has always been important to me and still is. Some of my best friends play for Lancashire and I try to catch as many County games as I can during the close season because if I had not made it at soccer I would have been happy to try my luck at cricket. The chance did come when I was invited to Old Trafford to join the ground staff, but it would have meant sacrificing my football to devote all my energies to the summer game and I was not prepared to do that. With hindsight I'm sure I made the right decision, but when you take eight wickets for three runs as a 12 year old it's inevitable that you do let your mind wander – if only fleetingly.

By the time I was 14 I was playing for Preston Schoolboys as an outside left, and the scouts were starting to turn up. I had the chance to go to Blackpool, Preston and West Ham at that stage, but my mum was always drumming into me the need to get my O levels before considering a professional career as a sportsman. I've been grateful for that advice all my life, and also for her steadying influence during my formative years. When the offers came in I discussed them with her. Really it was a straightforward choice once she gave her blessing. There was great rivalry between Preston and Blackpool and it would have been tantamount to treason to go to Bloomfield Road. And West Ham? Well that sounded like the other end of the world – after all it was in faraway London. My mum agreed that it should be Preston on condition that it did not interfere with my education. Jimmy Milne, a former Deepdale manager and the father of

Gordon Milne, was the man who invited me to Preston.

My stepfather was already a director of the club so we deliberately did not tell him I was going for some training sessions at Preston. Alan Ball senior was the manager at the time with Arthur Cox the coach. Neither of them knew of the family connection either. They both watched my first trial game and after 20 minutes Mr Ball stopped the action and called me over to the touchline. I was a bit nervous because I thought I had done something wrong, but in fact he invited me to sign schoolboy forms for the club. Again I discussed it with my mum before agreeing to sign and it was only then that we felt able to inform Mr Ball that my stepfather was one of the people he was working for! I would train with Preston during the holidays but did not commit myself until I had my O levels. At 16 I was ready but Alan Ball had been sacked.

Frank Lord took over as caretaker–manager while I was still a schoolboy player. He was a well-travelled centre forward in his playing days who had survived several serious injuries and operations to stretch out his career. His bravery and courage were his trademark and his stock phrase was 'Cowboys don't cry', clearly a reference to his experiences on the field. The young players at Preston had a little game of their own in those days. Preston's training ground was adjacent to the stadium and we would practise hitting the cross bar with shots from 20 yards. After a while we became quite proficient at it until one day Frank spotted us and decided to join in.

He spent an age attempting to hit the cross bar without success before storming off in a foul mood. Perhaps we had got it wrong, after all in his business it was all about putting the ball under the bar and into the net. Frank left at the end of that season despite keeping Preston out of the Third Division. I think he felt he had done enough to get the job on a permanent basis but it was not to be.

Arthur Cox, who has remained a friend all these years, used to give me a hard time at training sessions to try and goad me into some kind of retaliation. I've always been placid by nature but Arthur would kick lumps out of me to get a reaction. I hated him at the time but I can understand it all now. Even when Derby were celebrating their return to the First Division last summer he still found time to ring me up to see how I was recovering from an operation to my Achilles' tendon. That's typical of the man and I'm pleased to see he is getting his rewards all these years later. His dedication is an example to everyone. In those early days I was so skinny you would find more fat on a greasy chip. Arthur put me on weight training to try and build me up but it has to be said that I'll never be a heavyweight no matter what I try.

Meanwhile, I was preparing for my A levels and an ex-soccer pro had come to join the school's staff. Eddie Brown played centre forward for Birmingham City before turning to teaching and just as Peter Singleton had influenced me earlier so did Eddie when he took charge of football. At 16 I was now a mid-field player probably because I did not have the physical strength to play up front.

A levels suddenly took a back seat when Bobby Charlton became the new Preston manager. Thanks to the expert guidance of Eddie Brown in the sixth form, football had become my consuming interest. I was playing in a practice match at Deepdale when I saw the great man walk to the touchline to get a closer view of the action. When it was over he offered me a contract to turn professional. If I hesitated it was because I was in total awe of him. I was 17 and he was, well, he was Bobby Charlton. Just to be in his company and to hear him speaking to me was more than enough. I often think back to that meeting because it was probably just as big a trial for Bobby as for me because he is a naturally shy man despite his worldwide reputation. But when he asked me to join Preston, A levels went out of the window and even my mum understood because she knew that I had set my heart on becoming a professional and the signs were looking promising.

Norman Bodell was Bobby's coach but he was also a part-time model, and when somebody at the club discovered some pictures of Norman advertising men's underwear and stuck them on the wall in the dressing room, he was not amused. It was like square bashing for the apprentices in those days and the boys from the YTS, who are the modern equivalents, have it very easy by comparison. We were expected to clean the boots of the professionals and keep the dressing rooms spick and span. We were never allowed to leave the ground until Norman had made his inspection and given us the all-clear. He would wet his finger and run it along the window-sills checking for dust. One summer he had us all on top of the main grandstand replacing broken tiles. It doesn't happen today.

The team would train at a place called Willow Farm which was exactly 2.6 miles from Deepdale. I know because I would run it every day. We would load up Bobby's Range Rover with all the kit, balls, cones and everything else needed for a training session and then run behind the Range Rover. When the session was over we would load it up again and run all the way back. But the football side was never neglected for us youngsters because Bobby believed in a youth policy, so I was in the Central League side at 17. I was still eligible for the Youth team at this stage but was suspended for a Youth Cup tie after collecting four cautions. It led to a row with Norman which I have never forgotten although we are pals whenever we bump into each other. The team was beaten in the Cup tie and Norman blamed me because I was banned. He gave me a ticking-off while he was sitting on the toilet. 'It's your fault we are out and the sooner you get your disciplinary record straightened out the better' was the message from behind the closed door. I resented that because as time has shown I have never had any serious problems on that score and I don't think my worst enemy in the game would accuse me of being a dirty player.

Playing for the reserves brought me into contact with Nobby Stiles, another big influence on my career. Nobby was player–coach and he was the first man to suggest that my future might lie in defence rather than any other position. We were 3–0 down at half-time against Aston Villa, and I was playing on the wing, when Nobby changed it all round for the second half and moved me to full back. We still lost 4–1 and it was Nobby who told me he didn't think I would make it as a winger. He said he saw me as a central defender and he started playing me there as often as he could for Preston reserves, even though that was his position in those days. It meant he did not turn out as regularly as he would have liked but that was typical of him. He is a 13 totally unselfish man who is always prepared to go out of his way to help people. The whole world remembers his dance of delight at Wembley when England won the 1966 World Cup and I think the nation adopted him when they saw his huge smile minus the teeth. As a coach coming towards the end of his playing career he gave me invaluable assistance and the benefit of his experience.

Like any good pro he hated to lose at anything. We had a gym at Deepdale where we would play a game of our own invention called Chippy. It was one against one and the object was to chip the ball over your opponent's head and strike the door to score a goal. Nobby could not resist having a crack at this but being such a small chap he found it difficult to avoid being lobbed as the ball passed over his head to register yet another goal. The upshot was that Nobby refused to allow any of these games to end until he had scored a few himself. And that meant some marathon sessions on more than one occasion.

Bobby Charlton brought me into the first team for the final three games of the 1975–76 season. My debut was at right back against Watford; I was only 17 and it was a tremendous thrill to be playing League football so early in my career. It brought me into closer contact with Bobby and I shall never forget one day when he was reading out the team sheet of our opponents and I noticed how his hands were shaking. So perhaps it was not a surprise when he left the job soon afterwards, never to try management again.

I don't think he needed all the hassle that goes with the job. As one of the all-time great footballers, I feel management imposed a strain on him, and he certainly seems a more relaxed figure whenever I see him these days. Bobby left because he objected to the board's decision to sell John Bird to Newcastle. Bird was a strong solid centre half but in return Preston were getting Alex Bruce, a proven goalscorer who had been a big favourite at Deepdale before moving to the North East. In my humble opinion the deal made sense, but Bobby made his stand over it and left. I can't be sure, but I believe he never regretted it.

In his place came a manager with a big reputation. Harry Catterick had won the championship and the FA Cup with Everton, and was regarded as a no-nonsense type who did not waste his time with people he did not like. I had heard various stories about him but he made a big impression on me when he addressed the players for the first time. As Norman had left with Bobby he promoted Nobby to first-team coach, which we all thought was a great move for the club. 'If you don't want to play for me there's the door' was Harry's opening remark. He came to watch me play in the reserves when I had the misfortune to strain knee ligaments which put me out for three weeks. But Harry came into the treatment room while I was receiving attention and told me that as soon as I was fit I would be in the first team. Is it any wonder I consider myself a pro-Catterick man? I knew however that there were other players at the club whom he would not even speak to.

With Nobby on first-team duty, goalkeeper Alan Kelly took charge of the reserves and that's how the great Irish adventure began. Alan, an Irish International of many years, discovered that my grandfather came from Waterford, and before I knew it I was being issued with an Irish passport and was in the squad to play Poland in Dublin. I had never even met the manager Johnny Giles; the first time I did was when I reported to the team's hotel. But the Irish experience is another story in itself and recorded elsewhere in this book.

Here I was, at 18, a fully-fledged international player from the English Third Division who had never set foot in the Emerald Isle before I received the call to wear the green jersey. I must have been shaping-up reasonably well because there was talk of my moving on to higher things. Ironically, one of the stories linked me with a transfer to Newcastle in exchange for John Bird, and Liverpool was also mentioned. When the move came, however, it was to the other end of the country for one of the happiest but most traumatic experiences of my life.

SEAGULLS AND LIVERBIRDS

I was on holiday in Benidorm with some of the Preston lads when the call came saying Brighton wanted to buy me. Their Chairman, Mike Bamber, was flying out to discuss the move and Preston was leaving the decision to me. I was a little the worse for wear because I had been enjoying the Spanish sunshine and the beer at the end of the season, but I still had enough common sense left to realise that Mr Bamber was teetotal and that it would not look very good if I was under the influence when he met me for the first time. He arrived with another Brighton director and checked into a hotel which cost around £14 a night. Before committing myself I insisted on talking to my stepfather back home in Preston, and my abiding memory of that occasion is of a frantic hotel manager trying to interrupt me to discover who was paying for the phone bill which would be considerably more expensive than a room in his hotel.

Eventually I signed a blank contract for Mr Bamber and celebrated the deal with beans on toast and orange juice in a Benidorm bar. The fee was £110,000 which made me Brighton's most expensive signing at the ripe old age of 19. Alan Mullery, the manager, was on holiday somewhere else in Spain but he contacted me to stress that he was the man behind the signing – he was putting his reputation at stake by investing so much money in me.

I loved Brighton as soon as I saw the place, bright, bustling and cosmopolitan, and the football club was on a high. They had just been promoted to the Second Division and everything was looking good. What I did not realise when I arrived was that I was taking the place of Graham Cross, the former Leicester player, who had enjoyed a tremendous season in Brighton's promotion run. There were a few mutterings in the dressing room about this unknown teenager from Preston but Alan Mullery soon silenced them and made it very clear that he was backing me to the hilt. It was the first time I had been away from home but it did not seem to matter. Most of the Brighton players had been recruited from different parts of the country and there were very few locals in the team. There were never any problems about settling in because the majority of the players were in the same boat so we tended to stick together.

I defy anyone not to like living in Brighton. I could see myself staying there permanently long after my football career was over, that's how much I liked the place, and it seemed that the club would be successful for a long time to come. We just missed out on promotion to the First Division in my first year, but it would happen 12 months later. The town was football daft and we were getting gates of 24,000 on a regular basis at the Goldstone Ground. The travel arrangements were a little different also. They had a train called the Seagulls Special which we used for all away trips. Some of the carriages came from the old Brighton Belle and these were assigned to the players, with the fans filling up the remainder of the train for the long journeys North. It really was a life of luxury, especially after the old team coach we had used at Preston. Here we were sitting in armchairs with a bell by our sides to ring for service as we travelled the country in style. And, as we were winning most of our matches, the return journeys quickly became one long party.

The only cloud on the horizon concerned my private life. At Preston I had met Ellie, a bright intelligent girl who was at teacher training college in Liverpool. We seemed to hit it off from the start so when my transfer came through to Brighton I needed to make a big decision. Did I leave Ellie behind or did we put down roots in my new home? At first I would travel back North at weekends to see her but I was being torn by the good life in Brighton. The success on the field and the enjoyment I got out of mixing with the boys at the club were not easy to ignore. It could not go on like that indefinitely, something had to give, and eventually I took the plunge and married Ellie just before my 21st birthday.

It's easy to say now that it was doomed from the start and I was too young to settle down. Within 18 months of meeting her we were married and living in Brighton. I take no pleasure in admitting that within a matter of weeks we were growing apart and I accept the responsibility. Brighton is such a lively place you can find something to do every night of the week if you wish, and I was being fêted everywhere I went which was no preparation for married life. I admit I enjoyed the hero worship – who wouldn't at my age? – and I just could not reconcile all that with sitting at home in my slippers playing the dutiful husband. In the end I suggested to Ellie that she returned North for a few weeks to see how we felt when we were apart. It may sound callous but I already knew the marriage was not going to work from my point of view. It was not Ellie's fault. She was a lovely happy girl, but the prospect of being married for life filled me with despair. I knew I had made a mistake, but how was I to rectify it without hurting people's feelings, not least Ellie's?

The most daunting task of my life was to explain to her and her parents that I wanted a divorce, just four months after getting married. Of course there were recriminations and some bitterness but I felt it was the right thing to do. Gary Williams, who had followed me from Preston to Brighton, had his ear bent non-stop during this very painful time before I took my problem to the club. Mr Bamber and Alan Mullery could not have been more supportive and put me in touch with an eminent barrister in London. In those days it took two years for a divorce to become absolute but on his advice I sought an early settlement with Ellie.

It cost me £14,000, which was a fortune to me, but Brighton lent me the money, another reason for me to be grateful to them. The pain was not all on one side. It was not easy explaining to my mother and stepfather, but I was very honest with them and admitted I had made a big mistake marrying so early with my football career just taking off. To be perfectly frank, football was everything to me and neither Ellie nor anyone else could compete with it. I repeat, the fault was mine and I am not proud of that episode in my life. Ellie has since re-married, ironically to a chap I know, and she lives in Brighton now. I genuinely hope she is very happy, she deserves to be.

After that unhappy chapter I met Vanessa, a dancer with Sacha Distel. We bumped into each other walking our dogs in a Brighton park and we have been together ever since. Vanessa went to a stage school in London and continued her dancing career for the first few years we were together, but now she has a full-time job looking after me in Southport!

After the traumas of the divorce, Brighton's success and the appearance of Vanessa helped me to pull myself together again and the club won promotion to the First Division. I was really in the big time now and I can rememer my first visit to Anfield when we lost 1–0 to an Alan Hansen goal and I had the doubtful privilege of marking Kenny Dalglish, the man who was to become colleague, next-door neighbour and eventually my boss.

That game was an experience in itself, because as I have always maintained, Kenny is the most difficult opponent I have ever faced, but there will be more about him at a later stage. We finished sixteenth that season but the following year the Brighton success story started to turn a little sour. The club had spent heavily to establish themselves in the First Division but we just missed relegation the following year. In the last game we played Leicester and needed a result to survive. We got it because they finished up with only nine men after Alan Young and Kevin MacDonald had been sent off. Kevin of course joined me at Liverpool later on but he got his marching orders that day for knocking me out. He still insists that it was an accident but I remember it as a flying head-butt from 20 yards!

At the end of that season there was more speculation about my leaving Brighton and I went to see Alan Mullery, who had always been straight with me, to ask him about the rumours. He said I would leave over his dead body, that I had a 10-year contract with the promise of a testimonial and that the club had no intention of selling me. But in the close season Alan left and I heard later that it was over me. Mike Bamber repeated they had no intention of selling me but Alan quit because he had heard the opposite. Mike Bailey came in as manager and made me captain. But he did ask me what I wanted to do which suggested to me perhaps my time was up at Goldstone. I don't know if there was a financial crisis and they were looking for a big transfer fee from my sale to sort themselves out but the uncertainty did unsettle me. I was sent off in a pre-season match, and I put it down to the frustration and the doubts about my future, because it is rare for me to get into trouble with referees. Mike Bailey must have sensed it too because the next day we had a meeting when we agreed it would be better if I left.

Arsenal were the first club to approach me and Terry Neill and secretary Ken Friar came to see me. Now they don't come any bigger than Arsenal and the prospect of playing for a major London club did appeal in one way, yet at the back of my mind I had reservations. Terry asked me to go to Highbury for further talks but I refused, because I felt that if I saw the set-up with the famous marble halls I would sign and might live to regret it later. Part of the deal involved Steve Gatting and John Devine moving from Arsenal to Brighton but that side of it fell through and I thought that would kill off the whole package. But Terry was persistent and was setting up an alternative deal when I received a telephone call from a journalist who was on a pre-season tour with Liverpool in Switzerland. He told me the European champions were interested in me but at that stage I had heard nothing about this. His information must have been good, however, because some hours later his tip was confirmed, and I was due to meet Bob Paisley.

Just to complicate matters further Ron Atkinson, who was in the process of signing Frank Stapleton from Arsenal, made his interest known and implored me not to sign for anyone until I had spoken to him. Arsenal, Liverpool and Manchester United, talk about being spoilt for choice! Perhaps I knew it was going to be Liverpool because I remember telling Ron that I could not promise to delay a move if I was happy with the club concerned and the contract on offer. I met Liverpool that night at a hotel near Heathrow. Bob Paisley, the Chairman John Smith and the Secretary Peter Robinson, were all involved. Terry Neill was in the hotel next door as Arsenal were preparing to fly out on a pre-season tour and he asked to be kept informed if I did not join Liverpool.

There was really no contest. Liverpool had just beaten Real Madrid in Paris to win the European Cup again, and the prospect of playing for the most successful team in the country was too good to turn down. I signed within 20 minutes of meeting the Anfield officials, and told Terry of my decision. I never got back to Ron but really there was no need. When he heard the news I'm sure he would have remembered our earlier conversation and realised my mind was made up. In fact I was 90 per cent certain to sign for

Liverpool before I spoke to them and I have never had any reason to regret my decision.

My first season at Liverpool coincided with a big team shake-up which does not happen very often at Anfield. Bruce Grobbelaar took over in goal from Ray Clemence and it was a big breakthrough for players like Craig Johnston, Ronnie Whelan and a certain Ian Rush. Clem, Jimmy Case and Colin Irwin had moved on as Bob Paisley reshaped the team following the latest European success.

The first few weeks for a new boy are always a bit nerve-wracking. You are careful what you say until you get to know everybody because the last thing you want to do is to start off on the wrong foot. My first meeting with the Liverpool lads was at Gatwick Airport en route to a pre-season game against Atletico Madrid. I made sure I was early and waited around for 40 minutes for the main party to arrive.

The first thing that struck me was the informality of it all. Joe Fagan was in charge of the hotel accommodation and ordering the meals, and the first question he asked me was what I would like for my dinner in Madrid. I was rooming with Phil Neal, because Clem had been his regular partner for a number of years and Phil needed a new companion just as I did. We stayed together for most games after that. It's all about finding somebody who shares similar habits. Both Phil and I like our sleep so it suited both of us if the lights went out around 11 pm.

Terry McDermott, the real joker at Liverpool in those days, was on the trip and asked me if I was nervous as we prepared for our first training session. He then pointed to his pal Alan Kennedy and said 'I shouldn't worry, nobody could look as bad as Alan did when he first arrived.' I had some idea what to expect from Terry because his reputation had travelled before him.

He must have been some kind of superman because he could drink lager until the cows came home during the week (and never put on an ounce of weight) and then go out and run non-stop for 90 minutes at the weekend. Don't ask me how he did it, because in training you would never have guessed he had so much stamina. I doubt if the training staff at Anfield knew the answer either. Terry was always up to something. After one weekend we reported back for training 21 and Terry was very coy as he changed into his gear but we still noticed several stitches in his backside. 'I went to a party on Saturday night and a coffee table collapsed underneath me', was the explanation. True or false? With Terry you never knew for sure. When he moved on to Newcastle we bumped into him again before a Friday night Cup tie on television. Terry had a sore on his lip – he was not a pretty sight – so Graeme Souness decided to set him up. Goodness knows where he got them from, it must have been from one of those joke shops, but he managed to find a load of stick-on sores, which he handed out to the team. We all sported them for Terry's benefit – that's the type of humour he appreciates.

I started my Liverpool career at left back. Bob Paisley pointed out that Phil Thompson and Alan Hansen had done well as central defenders the previous season and although he knew this was the position I favoured he was also prepared to take advantage of the fact that I played in a number of positions. That was fine with me, at least I was starting in the team. I knew that better players than I had been forced to play in reserve-team football when they first arrive at Anfield, and just because I was the record buy didn't guarantee me anything and I knew it.

Right from the start I saw it was different at Liverpool from what I was used to at Brighton. You were never fined if you were late for training. Nobody made a habit of it, of course, but unlike Brighton they were not clock-watchers. All Bob Paisley would say was 'Be ready to leave for training by 10.15'. It was clear from the start that you were treated as an adult and you were expected to behave like one – even Terry Mac. There were no factions, everybody joined in and Kenny Dalglish even took me house-hunting in Southport. He doesn't stand on ceremony now he's manager as I discovered in the summer when he knocked on my door to introduce me to John Barnes who had just arrived from Watford.

I had been sent off at Brighton in a pre-season game just before my transfer to Liverpool, but had not mentioned it because I did not want anything to jeopardise the move. I was not expecting any disciplinary action because it had been in a friendly so it came as a tremendous shock when the UEFA report came through with a two-match ban. 'Don't you remember getting sent off?' asked Bob Paisley. He clearly knew all about it and perhaps I had been naïve to think such a professional outfit as Liverpool would not have done their homework.

I received my only sending-off with Liverpool in that first season in a European Cup tie against CSKA Sofia in Bulgaria. It was a bad day all round for Liverpool. Bruce made one costly mistake for a goal, Ian Rush had a legitimate one disallowed and I got the red card for doing nothing at all.

It came in a goalmouth scramble when Liverpool hit the bar and the ball was scrambled away. It went straight to a Bulgarian and I got in a perfectly fair tackle which the referee obviously thought was OK, too, because he waved play on. But the next second my foreign friend went down pole-axed clutching his face and I was given my marching orders for a magnificent piece of acting. If they give Oscars in Bulgaria he was a prime contender. Significantly when the Bulgarians sent over a tape of the game, my sending off and Rushie's disallowed goal had mysteriously disappeared from the recording.

We won the championship that season and the Milk Cup against Spurs and, although I had appeared in a variety of roles, I only missed five games so I was more than satisfied with my first year at Anfield.

THE GLORY THAT WAS ROME

Joe Fagan sings Chris Rea! That was just one of the highlights of Liverpool's European Cup triumph in 1984. Just as Heysel will be imprinted on our minds for all the wrong reasons, so that night in Rome will rank as the outstanding good memory of the competition for me. It will never be repeated, because after the scenes which followed our win on penalties, UEFA decided that the final will never again be staged on the ground of one of the competing clubs.

It was a fantastic season for Liverpool (and Joe Fagan's first in charge), and we ended it with three trophies; the championship, Milk Cup and Europe's top prize. While the double will always remain a special part of Liverpool's history the more I think about that treble the more I think it deserves to be bracketed with the double.

The European campaign was extraordinary because we won so many of our away games. That's really doing it the hard way. The normal practice is to try and win at home, and keep a clean sheet, then put up shop on the away trip, but we just could not stop scoring goals on our travels. Don't ask me why it happened, but the further we went in the competition that year the more confident we were that we would score goals no matter how tough it might get. And believe me, it did get very tough, particularly in Bucharest and in the final.

When we beat the Rumanians to ensure our place in the final we knew it was going to be something entirely different, a one-off against Roma in their stadium. There was a long gap between our winning the championship, and having to play in the final, so Joe decided to take us away to Israel. Normally we go there at the end of the season, when perhaps we do not do ourselves full justice because it is considered a holiday – but not in the spring of 1984. Joe picked Israel because we were always comfortable there, and because the climate would be similar to what we could expect in Rome. That is why we trained so hard in Tel Aviv and it showed in the game when we beat the national side 4–1.

We were so fired up for the final that Joe had to apply the brake in training, that's how keen we were, even though everything was stacked against us. Joe was worried that somebody might get injured in training because we were going at it so hard, and that's unusual for Liverpool. But then the whole build-up and circumstances were totally different for this game. We were all aware that this was unique; to go into somebody's backyard to bid for the most coveted prize in Europe.

There is a very good pop singer who hails from the North East, called Chris Rea. We got to know his music through Craig Johnston and David Hodgson who knew him from their Middlesbrough days. Craig was really keen on his music, but at the time Chris Rea was not a household name. However, when we won the European Cup even Joe Fagan knew the words of his song, which we claimed for ourselves for that special occasion, and today just about every player at Anfield will claim to be a Chris Rea enthusiast. For the record – excuse the pun – the song was called 'I don't know what it is but I love it'. Since then of course he has had a smash hit with 'Let's Dance' and the name of Chris Rea is known throughout the country. However, more of this later.

We were all in great shape for that final, and it's not often you can say that about the entire squad at the end of a season. Only Kenny Dalglish was a bit short of match practice, and he was still recovering from a fractured cheek bone he had suffered against Manchester United earlier in the season. He was our only worry because we knew we could not afford to be without him. We had a week to go before Rome when we returned from Tel Aviv, and again the training was very competitive and completely out of character for Liverpool who have their own way of preparing players and arduous work-outs are not part of the normal programme. We were not being pushed into it either, it was just a case of everyone getting very wound up at the prospect of what faced us in Rome. We were champing at the bit and, without anything being said, we knew that no matter what handicaps we faced, we were in the mood to claim a famous victory in Rome, the site of Liverpool's first European Cup win in 1977.

Liverpool kept everything as near to normal as possible

and we didn't set off until the day before the match. We knew that if the game went into extra time and there was still no result then a penalty shoot-out would decide the outcome, so we needed to select our five men to take the penalties. Nobody wanted that job because of the pressure that would be on the luckless five, but at the time we never imagined the game would go to penalties. If we had, the five nominated would probably have offered the job to someone else. The five 'volunteers' were Steve Nicol, Ian Rush, Phil Neal, Graeme Souness and Alan Kennedy, but with no pre-selected order of taking them. Before we left, we had a trial run with our five competing against some of the youngsters at Anfield and we lost 4–1! Not a happy omen but we decided to keep that result quiet until after the game. I remember Joe saying after that effort that we had better win it in 120 minutes at most.

When we arrived in Rome we soon got a taste of what was to come. We had arranged a training session on the Wednesday morning, and I can't believe that it was just a coincidence that the pitch assigned to us was one of the worst I have ever seen. If ever a surface was designed to cause problems, and possibly injuries, this was it. I wouldn't have taken my dog for a walk on it, let alone used it for a team of footballers. The surface was badly rutted and Joe warned us all to be careful, as if we needed any reminding, in view of the task that faced us later that day.

After lunch we had a team meeting and Joe informed us of a new directive from UEFA instructing players not to run towards the crowd if a goal was scored, because there was a danger of provoking what was going to be a very big and excited audience. Joe amended that when he read it out. 'When, we score a goal not *if*' and then added 'when we score our goals do as UEFA say for the first two but do what you like if we get any more.' It was a nice touch, because apart from demonstrating his confidence it helped to ease the inevitable tension which was beginning to build up.

I was rooming with Phil Neal, and we went for our customary pre-match nap in the afternoon. We woke around 4.30 pm and switched on the television to be confronted with scenes from the Olympic Stadium. One section was already packed with Roma fans hours before the kick-off. There was a mass of Italian flags, and even at that stage firecrackers and flares were shooting into the sky. We both looked at each other and thought, this is going to be some night.

It was very warm but, conforming to our tradition, we were obliged to wear a suit and tie to travel to the stadium. We arrived earlier than usual because we didn't want to get snarled up in the traffic, but instead of heading straight for the dressing rooms Joe told us to go out into the stadium and give the backroom staff time to get our kit organised.

There was a schoolboys' game in progress and after watching this for about 10 minutes from the touchline some of the lads were ready to drift back inside. The Roma fans were already shouting and screaming because they had recognised us. Goodness knows how long they had been there, but by this time they were working themselves up into a frenzy.

That's when Graeme Souness pulled his master stroke. He was lapping it all up because the greater the hostility the more he likes it, and he suggested that we walk around the ground. Naturally, when we approached the Roma section their fans went crazy, calling us every name under the sun, Italian style, but what it did for us was to bring everybody even closer together. We had our own supporters inside the ground by now, even though they were considerably outnumbered. What the Roma fans did not realise was that the louder they screamed and shouted, and the greater the commotion they created, the more they revealed their anxiety about the game. After all, a ball had not even been kicked at this stage.

There is a long tunnel at the Olympic Stadium leading from the pitch to the dressing rooms and as we made our way towards it David Hodgson started singing the Chris Rea song, 'I don't know what it is but I love it'. Gradually we all joined in, so as we passed Roma's dressing room the words and music were echoing down the corridor, almost like a chant. It was purely spontaneous and not designed to unsettle Roma. However, after the match their manager explained at the press conference that one of the worst things that had happened that night was to hear Liverpool players singing as though they hadn't a care in the world, while he was giving his men a pep talk and pointing out 27 how important it was for them to win, especially as they were the home team. I don't know if it was the quality of our singing he was referring to, or the fact that we completely threw his men because we seemed so relaxed. Such insignificant moments can have a tremendous impact on the biggest of games.

When the action finally started, Phil Neal gave us an early lead, but Roma equalised just before half-time. There were no more goals in the 90 minutes so we went into extra time, with the dreaded penalties now looming larger with every second that went by. We felt we were the stronger side at this stage, but we could not get the second goal which would have spared everyone the agony of penalties. The moment arrived when spot kicks were going to decide it.

We were all standing in the centre circle and I remember looking at Roma's nominated five and thinking that the odds favoured them because they had so many experienced men available such as Falcao, Conti and Graziani. I don't know if Joe felt the same way but he said it was all in the lap of the gods now. He told us that he couldn't have asked for any more from us, which suggested that he was not too confident about the outcome either. He added that drawing with Roma in their stadium made us the moral winners of the game no matter what happened in the shoot out, but it's fair to say that we were filled with apprehension about what was to come.

We were so full of our own thoughts that we barely considered Roma, yet when you look back at it the pressure was even greater for them. Steve Nicol, one of the youngest and least experienced players in our side, asked to take the first one so he could get it over with, and, of course, he missed, so immediately we were trailing. Phil Neal, Graeme and Rushie all scored for us, but I still feared the worst. I could not watch when it was the turn of Conti and Graziani because I was so sure they would score. They were World Cup performers and with all their experience I could not imagine them missing.

I was one of the few people in the stadium who didn't witness the extraordinary antics of Bruce when he pretended he was a bag of nerves and had an attack of the shakes as he stood on his goal line. It was a brilliant piece of

28

improvisation and typical of Bruce, and it certainly worked because they both missed. Suddenly, we were in the position of being able to win if Alan Kennedy converted our last kick, but in all honesty, I didn't think he would score. He was not renowned as a penalty expert, and whenever he got within sight of the opposition's goal Alan loved to blast the ball as hard as he could, and that applied to his crosses, too.

Alan, however, seems to make a speciality of winning European Cups. He had scored a spectacular goal against Real Madrid in Paris the season before I joined the club. That was another full-blooded effort, which even today the lads are not sure about. Was it a centre or a shot? It doesn't matter, of course, because it went in and won the Cup. But with a hostile crowd watching, and millions glued to their television sets throughout Europe, Alan confused everybody by calmly walking up and side-footing the ball into the net, as if he had been doing that kind of thing all his life. I can't remember Alan ever taking another penalty kick for Liverpool but that one was worth more than money could buy. We all went slightly crazy at that moment and the Chris Rea song was our signature tune again, although in the bedlam I'm sure nobody heard us singing.

We had a magnificent party that night at a sumptuous villa overlooking Rome. It was out in the hills and the last word in luxury. Even the drive seemed to stretch for a couple of miles once we turned off the road. Whoever organised it – I think Crown Paints, our sponsors, were involved – they certainly came up trumps. We were all together with our wives and girlfriends, and splendidly isolated so we could let our hair down and celebrate without any prying eyes.

The party went on until dawn and when we arrived at the airport for the flight home the ravages of the night must have been apparent. I won't forget my hangover, that's for sure. There was a delay getting away because a couple of the skips had been mislaid and we realised why when we eventually touched down at Speke. They were plastered in Italian graffiti, doubtless a parting gift from the baggage handlers in Rome who wanted to let us know exactly how they felt about the result.

That win was the climax of another remarkable season and I doubt whether any other English side will ever win the European Cup in such an exciting way. We actually won it in Europe!

In the first round we had beaten the Danish club Odense home and away; in the second round, after a goalless draw at Anfield against Athletic Bilbao, we won in Spain with an Ian Rush goal. In round three we had to settle for a 1–0 win, Rushie again, against Benfica at Anfield, but then won 4–1 in Lisbon. In the semi final Dinamo Bucharest held us to a Sammy Lee goal at home, but two more from Rushie in Rumania carried us through one of the most difficult and antagonistic games of my career.

With all due respect to Odense, we always anticipated an easy first round draw because as a seeded team we would have to be very unlucky to catch a sticky one right at the start. They held us to a Kenny Dalglish goal in Denmark but we put five past them at Anfield with Michael Robinson claiming two of them.

Bilbao was a different proposition. Very experienced and capable, they put up the shutters at Anfield and thought they had done the hard work by getting a draw. Their players were celebrating on the pitch when the whistle went, just as Bayern Munich had done in 1981 before Liverpool went out there to win the tie away from home. We knew we had it all to do in the second leg. They call the Bilbao stadium the Cathedral, and the Basque fans are amongst the most committed in the game. The ground is compact, with the crowd close to the touchlines and the grandstands bank steeply creating a cockpit atmosphere, just like Anfield. The British press had written us off which was the best thing that could happen, because that is like a red rag to a Liverpool player. We always respond on the few occasions when we are told we have no chance and, although I say it myself, we gave a superb display in the second leg. Bilbao never looked like scoring and Rushie won it for us with Alan Kennedy getting into the act by supplying the right foot cross, another rare sight, because Alan usually reserves that one just for walking on.

The Spanish fans, always pro-British in the Basque region, gave us a marvellous ovation at the end and that doesn't happen very often on our foreign travels. Joe Fagan played a major part in that victory, too, with some smart tactics.

After the first leg, the Bilbao coach was extolling the virtues of Craig Johnston and pin-pointing him as the danger man. Whether he had something up his sleeve or not we could not be sure, but he wrote a long article on Craig saying that if it were possible Craig would be the one Liverpool man he would like to sign. Joe sensed that the coach might be up to something, possibly playing two attacking men down our right flank, so at the very last moment he left out Craig and played Steve Nicol in Craig's position. Steve, an international full back, was clearly preferred because of his defensive capabilities but it must have come as a shock to Bilbao, and we like to think it threw their pre-match plans into confusion. Howard Kendall is their manager now and I am sure he will respond to the Basques and their love of football. They are certainly one of the most sporting crowds I have ever played in front of.

After beating Benfica 1–0 at Anfield we faced another tough hurdle in the second leg, but the trip to Lisbon started off like a holiday because we were based at Estoril. No wonder it is such a popular resort; it's one of the most attractive locations I've seen in Europe. When we arrived the weather was good, but on the night of the game the rain came down in buckets. That didn't stop a full house packing the famous Stadium of Light. It was my first visit to Benfica's home and the memory of seeing those thousands of rain-soaked fans covering a massive bank of the ground as we came onto the pitch remains one of the highlights of my career. It was also a great night for Liverpool. We cashed in on mistakes made by Benfica's keeper to romp away with the second leg 4–1.

After the game, Graeme, Bruce, Alan Kennedy and I went to one of the famous fish restaurants to celebrate. The adrenalin was still flowing through me so I settled for soup, plaice and a few beers. The other boys tucked into lobster and the other specialities of the house and when the bill came it was £60 a head, but there were no complaints from me. It seemed cheap at the price after our performance, because we knew that apart from Odense, we had removed two of the biggest names in the competition and another European Cup triumph was beginning to look possible.

The semi final always promised to be eventful. Dinamo

Bucharest were rated as one of the best teams to be produced in Rumania, and the whole country was behind them as the belief grew that they were destined to be the first team from that country to win the European Cup. It was obvious, right from the start of the first leg at Anfield, that they had come for a goalless draw, or at worst a single goal defeat. Most teams adopting these tactics can be relied on to use one lone striker, but there were periods in that game when Dinamo did not even bother to leave one guy up front on his own. They closed down space, used man for man marking on Graeme and Rushie and made it very difficult for us. Sammy Lee was the only one who managed to get through, but even at one goal down the Rumanians were quite happy to keep stonewalling. We were pushing hard for a second goal when the whole thing erupted.

We gained a corner at the Kop end and when the ball was eventually cleared one of the Rumanians was lying in the penalty area clutching his face. To be honest, I didn't see what had happened, and when I noticed him, there was nobody near him, but the Rumanians were in no doubt that Graeme was the culprit. Apparently, the Rumanian had suffered a broken jaw, and whatever the circumstances it made Graeme a marked man for the second leg.

Everyone in Britain knows what a tough character Graeme is, but although he later admitted in his autobiography that he was the man responsible, I don't believe he would inflict such a serious injury on anyone just for the hell of it. A lot goes on in matches which the public doesn't see, but whatever the rights and wrongs of this particular event, we knew we were going to need all our experience in Rumania, because the second leg was being whipped up into a grudge match with Graeme the number one target.

If ever a game was designed to show the true mettle of Graeme this was it. We had seen enough of Dinamo in the first leg to realise that we were in for a physical battle. At Anfield they didn't take any prisoners, coming in with late tackles and chopping people down from behind. With the scoreline so close and emotions aroused over the injured player, Bucharest was definitely not the place to be if you were wearing a red shirt that particular night.

We soon discovered what was in store for us when we

went to the ground on the morning of the match for our usual work out. It had been raining from the moment we arrived in Bucharest, a non-stop downpour which did not bode well against a team which specialised in flying tackles and a physical approach. Our first warning came on the team bus. There are always plenty of soldiers in and around football grounds in Eastern Europe and as our coach arrived it was immediately ringed by members of the armed forces. The bus was crawling very slowly through them when they started banging on the side of the bus. This was something new but we soon realised what was happening. As the knocking increased we looked out of the windows to see what they were up to. That's what they wanted because they were looking for Graeme and trying to catch his attention. When they did, it all became clear as they signalled what was in store for him, drawing their fingers across their throats to signal that Graeme was the prime target for some dirty business that night.

One becomes used to intimidation in football, but this was different. Graeme knew they were out to get him, yet he handled it impressively. Joe warned us in our team talk to be on our guard because there was going to be provocation of the worst sort and if we joined in it would suit Dinamo. You never know how a referee will react in those circumstances and no matter now strong willed he may want to be, the intimidation affects him, too. Joe stressed that a one goal lead was not so slender, as we knew from previous games, and the onus was on them to come at us. If we could get another goal and maintain our amazing record in Europe that season, the tie would be running in our favour.

The rain had never stopped and when we went out for our pre-match kick-in we were greeted by a storm of booing and whistling. You could feel the animosity sweeping from the terraces. There was hardly any cover in the ground but that had not stopped the Rumanian fans from filling the place hours before the kick-off. They were hoping to witness a public execution and Graeme was the man in front of the firing squad. It was clear that all the Dinamo team were programmed to try and nail him.

Everytime Graeme touched the ball in the kick-in, the crowd went wild, and it was obvious that every pair of eyes was focused on him – and Graeme knew it. I doubt if any player has been subjected to quite such a personal test in football. I don't know how I would react if I was ever placed in similar circumstances, but after watching the way Graeme handled it I like to think he set an example we could all copy.

I don't believe any other player from anywhere in the world could have handled this little lot as competently as Graeme did. What the fans didn't realise was that by concentrating all their vocal energy on Graeme they were winding him up and he thrives on that kind of thing. If they had got behind their own team instead of watching Graeme's every move, they could have made it more difficult for us. Mind you, it was difficult enough for us. One of the things about Liverpool has always been that we play as a team and if it's a backs-to-the-wall situation, as this undoubtedly was, we play for each other with even more commitment.

Graeme knew he was not alone, even though he took some fearful abuse when the game got under way. In the first 10 minutes one guy trying to make a name for himself came in with a deliberate leg breaker of a tackle. Graeme saw it coming just at the last moment and managed to escape serious injury, but there was a gaping hole in his sock just as a reminder that there was a long way to go and that there were some mean characters tracking his every move. Before half-time his shin pads were no longer in one piece either, but Graeme had set us on our way by then. It was a brilliant goal from Rushie – how many times will I say that in this book? – but it was supplied by Graeme, who was still managing to play an effective role in the game despite all the hassle and downright hatred which was coming his way.

Dinamo equalised before half-time from a dubious free kick to put them level on the night. We were still in front on aggregate and could even allow them to score again and go through on the away-goals rule, but Joe's half-time talk was blunt and clear – don't let them get another goal whatever you do. Play possession football because if we have the ball they can't possibly score. We did better than that with another goal from Rushie, supplied by Ronnie Whelan and we were through to the final. Nobody crows about victories at Liverpool but we all sensed this was a very special result and we were entitled to feel proud of ourselves.

It was Joe who gave it away when we dragged ourselves through the rain back to the comparative peace of the dressing room. Everyone was on a high with the adrenalin flowing, and Bobby Robson, who was on the trip to take a look at the Rumanians' technique, congratulated all of us and said he would be more than satisfied if his team performed as well in those circumstances. Joe summed it up best. He clapped his hands for silence and stopped the celebrations with a booming yell. It's not often he does things like that and we all wondered what was the matter. He jumped on the dressing room table and let loose an enormous cry of joy. We had never seen him do anything like this before, but it was his way of telling us that this was a one-off situation and to have come through it successfully and in one piece represented a mighty achievement even by Liverpool's high standards.

I'm sure other British clubs have stories to tell of outstanding results in Europe but I defy any of them to emulate what we achieved in Bucharest that day. Certainly, no individual could have handled it better than Graeme Souness. He was always 'Champagne Charlie' to the lads in the dressing room because of his extravagant life style, but take it from me, when the chips are down and you are relying on real men to get you out of trouble the first person you should look to is Graeme. If they had served the real thing in Bucharest he could have had champagne by the bucketful that night because he certainly earned it.

Of all the goals Rushie has scored for Liverpool, the one that took us through that night stands out for me. Apart from being one of the most important, it was sheer perfection in its execution, too. He chipped the keeper and the ball seemed to take an age to cross the line, but it was a perfect example of the man's uncanny ability when it comes to finishing. He knew exactly what he was doing and there was no way anybody was going to stop the ball from going in – I just wanted it to get across the line a bit quicker that was all. I should have known better, because when Rushie gets into those situations he is in total control and he probably knew it was going in long before any of us did.

On reflection, after our experience in Bucharest is it any

wonder that we went to Rome feeling we could handle any team, even in their own backyard? When English teams return to Europe – and the sooner that happens the better – it will take something out of the ordinary to match what Liverpool achieved that season.

THE BRUSSELS DISASTER

Everyone who was old enough claims they can remember exactly where they were and what they were doing when they heard the news of the assassination of President Kennedy in Dallas. It was such a shattering event.

I suspect in years to come no one who was at the Heysel Stadium in Brussels on 29 May 1985 will ever forget it; it will be imprinted on their minds forever. That disaster has been well recorded but each of us in that stadium has a story to tell and I am sure they will differ in some detail. I am no exception. What all the Liverpool players on duty that day have in common is the feeling of shock, and although it took time for the full significance to sink in we will carry that experience with us for the rest of our lives. Tragically, 38 others who were present will not.

Perhaps the omens were bad right from the start; I was rooming with Phil Neal the evening before the game, and we both settled down for a good night's sleep with lights out earlier than usual. This was the game billed as the clash of the champions; it was the match all Europe wanted to see and it seemed we were predestined to meet in the final from the beginning of the competition that season. We were the top team in Europe, and the holders of the trophy. Juventus believed they had their best ever team, and the European Cup was going to be theirs for the first time.

There was a massive build-up to the game. The publicity and excitement generated matched anything the competition had ever known even in those heady days when Real Madrid were the masters of Europe. We knew that if we won the trophy would become our property for all time, and as we had drawn a blank in domestic competition this game represented our last chance that season to win a prize.

There were a few problems in the build-up to that terrible day. I knew I needed an operation on my shoulder but I was confident I would be able to get through this final match. Ian Rush damaged his wrist in training and, although he was in pain, we knew he would be playing because he was so important to us. And Paul Walsh had been complaining about a stomach injury in the weeks leading to Brussels but he also knew he was expected to play.

The day started early. Phil and I had breakfast in our room and tuned into English television to hear a report that Joe Fagan, the manager, was retiring. We knew nothing about this, although it later transpired that the decision had been taken some months before. We didn't know whether to believe the story or not, and reported with the rest of the lads for a morning training session. Joe was in charge as usual and nothing was mentioned about his leaving although we all sensed something was going on. After lunch we had a team meeting and Joe said, 'After tonight you can call me Joe'. He had always been the boss to us so we drew our own conclusions. We didn't know if he was leaving, retiring or being moved upstairs but it created a bit of uncertainty straight away, and I think he was upset that the news had leaked out on the morning of a game like this. It was not the best time to hear something like that, but we were determined to put it behind us and get on with the game.

On the way to the stadium everything seemed normal. From our coach we could see Liverpool and Juventus supporters drinking together in pavement bars and enjoying themselves with improvised football games on any spare patch of parkland. It all appeared perfectly all right with no undercurrent or suggestion that it was going to go terribly wrong. When we arrived at the Heysel Stadium we had a little walk around the place and a chat with some of our fans, standard procedure before any Cup final for Liverpool.

We went into our dressing room to get ready when all of a sudden there was a tremendous roar from outside and a massive thud. One of the lads came running in, it was either Bruce Grobbelaar or Craig Johnston. The story was that Liverpool fans had charged the Juventus fans and a wall had collapsed. Immediately the boss ordered everyone inside and closed the dressing room door, saying that whatever may have happened we had to prepare ourselves for the game.

Then a crowd of riot police came charging through our dressing room. I haven't a clue how they got in and at the time we didn't know where they were going but it was clear that something was seriously wrong. Next, a stadium official came in and said there had been some trouble outside and that the kick-off would be delayed. Some of the lads started playing cards to pass the time and to take their minds off the match because we didn't know when it would start, assuming it would start at all.

A UEFA official was the next visitor and he asked Joe to go out with him and appeal to the crowd for order. We had our own regular minder with us, Tony Chinn, and he accompanied Joe onto the perimeter of the pitch. Apparently Joe got a lot of abuse when he appeared, which we could not understand, but we didn't know at the time the scale of the disaster. Then the UEFA official called for Phil Neal, our captain, to address the fans over the tannoy system and to appeal for order. By then we were all beginning to realise something terrible must have happened and if anyone from UEFA had come in and said the game was off we would all have been very relieved. We learnt later that Juventus wanted it cancelled but Liverpool argued it should go ahead to prevent even worse crowd trouble. On reflection that made sense but at the time we had other matters on our minds.

We had our wives, girlfriends and families in the ground and we knew many of them were located in a section of the grandstand close to where the wall had collapsed, immediately above our dressing room. Someone made enquiries for us and assured us they were all right. When we eventually came out onto the pitch the first thing we automatically did was to look to where the wall was supposed to be. We still did not know the magnitude of the disaster but by then we didn't really need to be told, we could sense it. I looked to the place where Vanessa and my stepfather were sitting, spotted them and knew they were safe.

When the game eventually started my shoulder went with my very first tackle. I knew it was dislocated without anyone having to tell me so I signalled to the bench that I was out of action, with just one minute gone. To be honest I felt a fraud. I knew I was taking a chance playing but I had thought that I could get through the game and face the operation afterwards. Coming off, I was in tears, something unusual for me, but I think everything had affected me by then, not just my injury, but the events before the game and my concern for my family in the stadium. It all became too much.

They took me to the dressing room and the Liverpool club doctor tried to put my shoulder back in. But it is almost impossible to do that with an athlete when he is conscious because the muscles automatically tighten up and my shoulder just wouldn't go back. Anyone who has suffered that type of injury will know how painful it is and I pleaded with the doctor not to keep trying because there was no way he could get it back. Tony Chinn had come down with me – he is a martial arts expert – and I feared he was going to attack the doctor whom he thought was hurting me.

The doctor suggested that I lie face down on the treatment table and hold a carton of milk in my hand because by swinging my damaged arm while gripping the carton it was possible the shoulder would slip back on its own. While this was going on, the half-time whistle went and the lads trooped in to see me swinging a carton of milk, face down, and Tony Chinn poised to spring like a cat at the doctor. As if enough was not going on without being confronted by this bizarre sight. Very little was said in the dressing room at half-time; I think all the lads were just counting the minutes to get through the second half so they could leave this sad place.

An ambulance came to collect me and take me to hospital. Tony Chinn carried me to it because I was in so much pain. I was still in my red Liverpool kit and when we arrived at the hospital they put me on a conveyor belt which carried me for at least 30 yards right into the interior of the building. The next thing I knew I was lying on a table with a mass of lights above and doctors rushing about. It was then that I realised that this must be the hospital where they had brought all the casualties from the stadium, and my own difficult position became apparent. I knew the Liverpool fans were being blamed for starting the trouble. I knew the vast majority of the admissions into this hospital were Italian, and I was still wearing my Liverpool shirt.

The hospital staff were marvellous, however. A surgeon who had been watching the game on television came straight over and said 'Mr Lawrenson, dislocated shoulder, right?'. He gave me an injection before attempting to put my shoulder back. The next thing I remember is waking up in a large empty room with an armed policeman guarding the door. In fact it was a 20 bed ward with just me in it. At first I didn't realise where I was and called out to the guy, who didn't speak English, but fortunately he called a nurse who did. She said 'You know what has happened don't you?' 'Sure', I replied, 'I've dislocated my shoulder.' 'I don't mean that', she added. 'The reason you are in an empty ward is because we have a lot of injured Italian people in this hospital. That is why there is a guard on the door.'

This was around 3 am and I drifted back to sleep for a few more hours. When I awoke again I had to be taken out to see the surgeon through a service lift, so that nobody would see me. The surgeon offered to do the necessary operation for me in the hospital but I told him I would need to go back to England and be guided by the club. He was a smashing guy. Despite all that was happening that dreadful night he still found the time to arrange for some breakfast for me and to feed me like a baby.

Later, 30 or 40 English, Belgian and Italian journalists arrived and started grilling me about the events of the previous night but there was little I could tell them. They tried to imply that it was a sick irony that I was in a hospital where some of the fans were undergoing surgery and others were actually lying dead; but what was I supposed to do about that? I had not asked to be brought to the same hospital although I was grateful for the first-class medical attention available.

When it was time to leave, Vanessa and Liverpool coach Roy Evans arrived with a change of clothing and hurried me out through another service exit to rejoin the team at their hotel. At least I was out of the Liverpool kit – who would ever think a football game could come to this? I did not know all the dreadful details until I met the rest of the boys, but I was catching up fast with the enormity of it all by the time we boarded the bus for the airport.

There were some Italian fans waiting as we left and one of them launched himself at the side of the coach. I am not likely to forget the sheer hatred etched on his face. At the airport it was the same, more Italian fans shouting insults and shaking their fists in rage. What could we say? What was there to say? All we could do was to leave with our heads down, feeling the shame of something we were not responsible for.

A year later I was to go back to Heysel to play for the Republic of Ireland. It was something I would have preferred not to do, but the first thing I noticed was that the dressing rooms had changed and when I looked around with the other Liverpool lads in the team, Ronnie Whelan and Jim Beglin, we saw that the wall had been changed too. So it was not as bad as I feared and in fairness we were met with kindness from all the Belgians we met. Perhaps it was a time for reconciliation – or at least for a step in that direction.

THE MEN WHO WON THE DOUBLE

Liverpool's 1985–86 double-winning squad was the equivalent of soccer's United Nations. I don't think there has ever been a British team with such a cosmopolitan look to it. England, Ireland, Scotland, Wales, Denmark, Zimbabwe, plus a South African-born Australian – all were represented. Since when has such a mixed bunch enjoyed such success?

The success isn't all down to playing ability either. A winning squad, working and living together for the best part of 10 months needs to get along on and off the pitch. If they don't, cracks will appear and tension will take its toll, particularly as Cup finals and championship deciders start to become a reality.

Like any other club, Liverpool is composed of vastly different types and we have our own interests away from the game, but put us all together and we seem to gel as a unit. We certainly did that great year of the double. When people ask what is the secret of Liverpool's enduring success, I suggest that it is the ability to get on with one another. I doubt whether outsiders have even given that a second thought. We have some of the biggest names in the game at Anfield, but none of them act like superstars. There are no ego trips because anyone getting on their high horse would soon be brought down to earth. We are one and the same when the whistle goes and that's the way it has always been at Anfield.

Let me be your fly on the wall in the Liverpool dressing room, and give you my own highly personal picture of the men who made it all possible. Anybody who has seen the team play will have formed their own opinions of the players, but it is their behaviour off the field which gives you a more precise picture of what makes them tick as individuals. Start from the premise that we are all slightly crazy and you are on the right lines.

Bruce Grobbelaar is probably crazier than anyone else, but then they say all good goalkeepers must have a screw loose, and Bruce is one of the best in the game. I rate him alongside Neville Southall as the most gifted in terms of ability. Bruce makes more mistakes than Neville because sometimes he is guilty of a lack of concentration, but he also stops shots no other keeper would get near. You are not going to change him at this stage of his career so occasionally you will see him stranded, coming for crosses which would have other keepers rooted to their line.

But we are talking about one of the most confident athletes I've ever seen. I deliberately use the word athlete rather than footballer because Bruce could have made a good living in a number of sports. He is a tremendous swimmer, loves keeping wicket at cricket and has a natural eye for any ball game. I have not seen anyone in any sport capable of throwing a ball as far as Bruce. He even has a little trick in which he can wind himself up and throw under arm probably as far as most of us can do over arm.

One day, when the weather was too bad for training at Melwood, we were switched to Anfield and Bruce turned up with a baseball bat and proceeded to smack a ball to all four corners of the ground. When we grew tired of retrieving it we sent him into the field and he left us all open-mouthed with a series of fantastic catches.

No goalkeeper has been so criticised for his mistakes, and I doubt if any other could have handled the criticism like Bruce but his highly independent streak allows him to take the knocks in his stride. I am not saying that he doesn't care, but he grew up early and he has had to stand on his own two feet for a long time. Can you think of another top-class footballer who fought in the African bush as a teenager before making a career for himself in England, via Canada? The vast majority came through the ranks as schoolboys, but by the time Bruce arrived at Anfield from Vancouver he had experienced more than many people would do in a lifetime. He came into the team at the same time as I did, and as new boys we had something in common. No wonder we have been mates ever since.

He is just as colourful off the pitch as on it; he is known for his spectacular clothes sense and occasionally outrageous head gear. He is also very much his own man. Abroad, players tend to go around together but if what Bruce has decided to do doesn't fit in with everyone else, he is quite happy to go his own way and join up with us later. In a café or bar he is usually the odd one out, ordering something totally different from the rest of us. He rooms with our other 'colonial', Craig Johnston, and although he is a practical joker himself he is not left out when it's his turn to be on the receiving end.

I set Bruce up on one occasion in London, getting a friend to ring him in his room claiming to represent one of the glossy magazines. He offered Bruce £10,000 to pose as a male model. The idea came from an earlier episode when the lads found a picture of Bruce in another magazine wearing just a pair of leopardskin shorts. That immediately went on display in the dressing room, but Bruce seemed happy enough so I set the next prank into operation. Bruce rang his wife Debbie at home, and when she said go ahead he agreed to do the non-existent session. We kept him hanging on for a couple of days before revealing it was all a leg-pull, and when he discovered I was behind it he almost ripped my head off. He would have happily modelled, so if any big magazine is looking for a well-known sportsman to display men's gear they know who to contact.

Bruce has established a special relationship with the Liverpool fans, who recognised early on that here was somebody completely different. When he says he came into football to enjoy it, that's exactly what he means and no matter what happens he is determined to do just that. That's why I'm sure he was sincere when he talked of quitting after Heysel. Bruce more than anyone regards football as just a game, and not simply a rewarding way to earn his living.

When he first arrived his nickname was 'Blue', then it developed into 'Blue Bayou', after the Roy Orbison hit record. More recently it has become 'Slaps', because Bruce is losing his hair rapidly, so it did not take long for 'Slaphead' to be abbreviated. Again, it's the least of his worries. If one of the lads asks him to pass the hair brush, Bruce will reply 'What would I be doing with something like that'. We won't get another one quite like him when he does move on.

Steve Nicol is another character. For a comparatively small fellow he has the biggest feet I've ever seen. He doesn't get his football boots from the usual people, he goes to Cammell Laird for a fitting! It's chips and crisps with everything for Steve, and I'm sure he would live on nothing else given the choice. He comes from Bill Shankly country in Ayr, so with his accent he was named 'Chops', because that's what it sounds like when he orders the inevitable plate of his favourites. It's hard to set him up because he has a nice line in doing it himself. He likes to tell the story of one close season when he was back in Scotland shopping with his wife, Eleanor. Steve was carting two full carrier bags around when he spotted some scales in the shop and jumped on them. He turned to his wife and said 'I've shot up to 13 st 10 lb'. He didn't realise that he was still holding the carrier bags.

He has a friend who runs a sports shop and on one visit his pal asked him to mind the store for a few minutes while he popped out. A customer came in wanting to buy a football, and Steve looked around and spotted one on the shelf. 'How much?' asked the guy. There was no price ticket on it so Steve needed to do some quick thinking. He knew at Anfield's souvenir shop they retailed at £6 but those balls are not the real thing, better suited for collecting autographs. '£6', said Steve and one satisfied customer walked out. When Steve's friend returned he asked if there had been any problems. 'No, and I even managed to sell a football' replied Steve. 'How much did you charge?' asked his pal. '£6', said Steve proudly. 'Those balls cost £40', said his furious friend – I don't think Steve has been behind his counter since.

One close season Steve and his wife teamed up with the Hansens for a summer cruise. It was on a big Russian ship and they were with some pretty high rollers. One night they wandered down to the casino where a game was going for big stakes. Alan and Steve joined in just for a bit of fun, not realising how serious the game was. A lot of the crew did not speak English, but the croupiers did, so Steve and Alan were able to get along. They were playing pontoon, and Steve was in the end place at the table. The croupier dealt a card out to each player and then asked them to place their bets. It was an international gathering and some of the players were old hands, well versed in the procedure and etiquette, but when it came to Steve's turn all eyes were on him as he flipped his second card over. The croupier looked at him to see what he was going to do, to be met with a rich Scottish burr saying 'I'm happy hen'.

On the same holiday a fancy dress competition was organised and Steve was invited to be one of the judges. On the big night he turned up in a grass skirt and layers of make-up, which according to Alan would have won him first place if he had been a competitor. Steve is everybody's friend and although he likes to tell stories against himself he is not fooling anyone. It's all a front and his way of getting a laugh, but underneath he knows what he is doing.

Jim Beglin was a very quiet lad when he arrived, and spent some time in the reserves before breaking through. He's from Waterford and has a broad Irish accent. It took some time to find a name for him because he kept himself to himself. Usually Alan Hansen comes up with the nicknames, and he duly found one for Jim. When he first came into the team he roomed with Alan, a move designed to settle him in. Before one big game Alan and Jim were watching *Dynasty* in their hotel room, and Dex Dexter was enjoying himself with Alexis. Alan turned to Jim and said 'That should be your game', and from that day on Jim has been stuck with the 'Dex' label. Don't ask me how but even some of the Liverpool supporters have heard about that and they call him Dex too. Alan sets the standard for these crazy names because he has been around longer than most of us and remembers when he was one of the younger members of the squad, and had the same things done to him by the senior players of the day. One of his best was to call Ronnie Whelan, 'Vitch'. Ronnie is also Irish and whenever he tried to say 'Just a minute' it came out as 'Dust a minute', so his first nickname was 'Dusty'. On one trip behind the Iron Curtain Alan was looking at the names of the team we were playing and noticed they all ended in 'vic'. 'If you were playing over here Ronnie they would call you "Dustyvic"' said Alan. That was it to begin with, but now it's been abbreviated to Vitch. Anybody who finds themselves in our company for the first time would be quite entitled to think he was with a bunch of lunatics, as these names get banded about, but each of us knows exactly who we are talking about.

As far as I know I'm still called 'Lorro'. As one of the older players I don't get exposed to as much mickey taking as some of the others.

Alan Hansen is commonly known as 'Norris', after the

compiler of the *Guinness Book of Records*, Norris McWhirter. Alan is our instant expert on facts, figures and statistics. If there is ever an argument about some sporting event which cannot be resolved because we don't have a reference book handy, the question always goes to Alan, because we know he will have the answer more often than not. His word is accepted as final, because it is rare for him to make a mistake. A little like his performance on the pitch really.

Alan is the master of the put-down. His sense of humour is so dry and dead pan that you cannot always be sure he is taking the rise out of someone. Alan is another natural sportsman; along with Gary Gillespie and Kevin MacDonald, he is the best golfer in the squad, and has also played squash for Scotland as a teenager. Being captain has given him added responsibility and he is regarded as the leader on and off the pitch.

When he was left out of the Scottish World Cup squad in 1986 by Alex Ferguson, none of the lads could believe it. Liverpool had just won the double and Alan had enjoyed a magnificent season. Typically, he didn't complain although I know he was desperately disappointed. All the lads and I were prepared to say exactly what we thought about that, even though Alan refused to get involved in a slanging match. To this day I can't imagine what Scotland were thinking of by leaving Alan behind. Playing alongside him for so many years I know what a good player he is and on the world stage I'm convinced he would have stood comparison with anyone.

On the golf course he drives the ball a prodigious distance, but like most of us these days, he doesn't have the time to give the game as much attention as he would like to. The close season in football seems to get shorter every year, and a day on the golf course has become something of a luxury.

When Kenny Dalglish was just a player he was known as 'Super', for obvious reasons. That became 'Sups' (pronounced Soops), because he was the star of the team even though he has never acted like one, despite being fêted everywhere he goes. Terry McDermott gave him that name when he spotted Kenny's mail one day; it would come by the sackful. This burden was passed on to Ian Rush when he emerged as the new king pin. I won't tell you what we call him now because he is the gaffer, but when we remember to we all call him Boss, at least to his face!

Craig Johnston, like Bruce, has an unusual background in football, and with it has come a stack of nicknames. His car registration was ROO 1, so he promptly became 'Roo' for starters. He had a spell as 'Skippy' and as 'Bottom Aussie'. He was taunted over that number plate, but he had the last laugh, because it was a valuable piece of property. Craig tells the story of being waved down on the motorway by another Australian who wanted to buy it from him there and then. The Bottom Aussie bit came when England thrashed Australia in the Test Series for the Ashes, Down Under, and when they lost the America's Cup the same summer. Craig is a big star in Australia, a household name, because they don't produce many footballers. We get at him by saying Tony Dorigo is the top Australian player in the British game, and Craig can quickly rise to the bait.

Like Bruce, he has achieved a lot in a short space of time. He made his own way over to England as a teenager to try his luck at football with Middlesbrough. He is a real globe trotter; the annual visit to Australia is just like a trip down the road for him these days because he has done it so often.

Craig is our unofficial club photographer. He takes it very seriously and anyone who has seen a selection from his portfolio will quickly realise why he is rated so highly in this subject. He has spent thousands of pounds getting all the very best cameras and equipment, and has a superb darkroom installed in his house which is the envy of many professional photographers. He always gets the call if any of the lads want pictures taken of their children, wives or girlfriends, because he is a real expert in this field.

Every Christmas we have a fancy dress party, which starts off at a Liverpool hotel, and Craig takes the official portrait for posterity. One year we all arrived in an assortment of gear and Craig spent a long time arranging us to get the best possible picture. When it was all to his satisfaction he got behind the camera but nothing happened. His expensive machinery had broken down. Any guest wandering through the hotel that night would have been mystified to see various pieces of costly camera equipment dotted around, and an

Australian guy sitting on the carpet muttering to himself 'That lens cost me a grand, and that piece was another grand ...'.

The fancy dress night has developed into quite an event, and I'll take some of the credit for that. The Brighton lads always had one, and when the Liverpool squad decided to have a Christmas bash they asked me what was the routine at Brighton. At first only half a dozen bothered to get dressed up, but now everybody joins in the spirit of it. After all, if you are going to have a party nothing gets you in the right mood faster than looking and acting the fool.

Ian Rush was called 'Tosh' in his early days. He was not renowned for his heading ability but one of his first goals for Liverpool was scored with his head so he was immediately named after John Toshack. Later Graeme Souness cruelly changed that to 'Omar', after the actor Omar Sharif, because Rushie's gear in those days was not exactly the height of fashion. Then he had his hair permed for a spell and got tagged 'Curly'.

Despite the cracks you could not put Ian down once he had established himself. He may have been a shy lad from North Wales when he arrived but today he has matured both as a person and as a player, and he is usually one of the instigators rather than a recipient when it comes to practical jokes. We are all sorry that he has left, but there is no resentment, just a little envy. He is an extraordinary player and he deserves all the rewards he can get. I'm sure he will be a great success in Italy, but I do wonder how he will cope with the life style over there.

Like the rest of us he likes a drink now and again, but in Italy if he is spotted in a bar it could easily be misconstrued. It will be like living in a goldfish bowl and that is something he has not encountered before. Of course he is a big star in England and Wales, but having a few pints with his mates in Flint doesn't arouse any interest, in Italy it will be a different story. At Liverpool his peg in the dressing room was next to mine and many times there was no room for me to sit down because of the volume of mail deposited for Rushie – that's a measure of his popularity and rightly so.

He may be a master footballer but when it comes to staying in a hotel he is the world's worst. He and Ronnie Whelan deserve each other. If you ever had the misfortune to go to their hotel room you would swear it had just been burgled. Nobody, but nobody, can make such a mess in such a short space of time, as those two. You will find plates all over the place, ice buckets, trays with bits of food on them, half-empty glasses and clothes flung everywhere. We say that they are the only two people who actually hang up their clothes on the floor. Within a matter of minutes of arriving anywhere their room looks as though a bomb has hit it. You would not believe it unless you saw it for yourself.

I've had the same experience in smaller doses, because I room with Ronnie on Ireland trips and I have never met anyone so scatter-brained when it comes to looking after his things. I can just picture his long-suffering wife following him around their house in Southport picking up things he has dropped, because I honestly don't think he realises it himself.

When we were playing a Cup tie at York one of my pals was due to collect a couple of tickets for the game. Ronnie told him to come up to the hotel room, and when the guy arrived and Ronnie opened the door he just stared wide-eyed. Some of us are more untidy than others but Ronnie and Ian are in a different league, and when Ronnie starts to shop around for a new room mate there will not be many volunteers – so be warned John Barnes and Peter Beardsley if he starts trying to persuade you as the new boys. He can't even be bothered to ring room service for himself, although he is pretty smart at asking you to do it for him.

Jan Molby lived closest to Rushie and they became friendly in Ian's last season. They formed a gang for fun at the club, admitting Steve McMahon to their exclusive little group because Steve rooms with Jan. Ronnie Whelan put up for membership, confident he would be elected because of his ties with Rushie, but he was black balled! He was made first reserve and when he was injured Paul Walsh applied for temporary membership, but was refused because his dress sense was rated dodgy!

When Jan arrived from Ajax, the Kop named him 'Rambo' because he is such a big fellow, and if you bump into him you're sure to finish up on your backside. The lads promptly changed that to 'Dumbo'! Now he is known as 'Yank', but nobody seems to know where that one came from. He is an amazing guy. He puts us all to shame when you think he speaks Danish, Dutch and English – even if it is with a Scouse accent. Funnily enough we don't notice it is Scouse, probably because we are with him every day. When I go down to Brighton to see old friends they reckon I have a Scouse accent, too, but I don't think I have. Maybe rooming with Steve McMahon is the reason for Jan's accent. It's the same as calling Paul Walsh a Cockney, when in fact he comes from South London, but once you get stuck with these labels it's not easy to lose them.

It's hard to believe that Jan is so young because of his size and the mature way he plays the game. I honestly believe he has everything it takes to become the most successful soccer import this country has ever seen, and I include Ossie Ardiles in that. If the true measure of success is the medals you have won, then Jan is already out in front. The best thing that ever happened to him was Kenny becoming boss, because he is clearly an admirer of Jan's play and has given him every encouragement.

When he first arrived he went straight into the team but then had a long spell in the reserves. I wonder how many single lads living in a foreign country could have handled that? He had to adjust to the English game, sweat off some weight and then fight to establish himself against fierce competition. He has done all of those things and there is more to come. If he lacks anything at all it is self-motivation, but when it comes to ability he has got it all. And for such a big man his touch and balance are quite extraordinary.

Ireland and Denmark were in the same qualifying group for the 1986 World Cup, and before we played Jan delighted in winding up Ronnie, Jim and me. In the end he had the last laugh because Denmark wiped the floor with us, particularly in Dublin. Rushie was getting some more of the same before he left for Italy because Denmark and Wales are in the same group for the 1988 European championships. We call Jan 'Fatty' if he really gets on our nerves, because he is such a big-boned fellow any increase in weight, even a few ounces, means he must get it off again quickly. Nobody is better qualified to help Rushie than Jan because he has been fending for himself ever since he left Denmark as a teenager. At least Rushie has Tracy with him, but Jan has done it all on his own so far.

Steve McMahon is known as 'Billy'. That name stems from a celebrity golf match that some of the lads played in Yorkshire. Big firms had put money into the event and their players were paired with various sportsmen and stars from the entertainment business. Steve went over with Alan Hansen and Gary Gillespie. When they checked the order of play to see who they were playing with Alan was linked with some representatives of a major business concern and so was Gary. But Steve was down to play with Billy Ingham and friends, so from that day he has been Billy in the dressing room.

He started off with Everton before joining Liverpool from Aston Villa, so it was inevitable that he took some stick when he first arrived, being accused of still having an allegiance to Goodison Park. It's not true, of course, and anyone who has seen him play in a Mersey derby will know that. Apparently when he was leaving Everton, Liverpool were ready to buy him, but the reaction was not good. He even had his car vandalised and felt he could not make the move across the city without becoming very unpopular. When he finally made it to Anfield nobody was more delighted than his father-in-law who has been a Liverpool fan all his life. He burst into tears when he heard the news, and today he likes to come along with Steve if a few of us are having a night out. That gives us more ammunition to have a chip at Steve, saying he is not allowed out on his own unless he has his father-in-law to look after him.

Gary Gillespie had to be called 'Dizzy' when he first arrived, but Alan Hansen decided that was too straight-forward and soon changed it. The boys were watching the Open golf championship on television and Ian Baker Finch was well up with the leaders. Gary turned to Alan and said 'This Ian Baker Smith has a real chance to win it'. Immediately Norris corrected him and from then on Gary became 'Smithy'.

He was very unlucky with injuries when he first arrived but such is dressing room humour that we would turn that into a joke too. 'Gary won't be playing this week because he has a slight cold' was just one of the wisecracks. One night, through no fault of his own, Gary didn't buy a drink which didn't go unnoticed, and the usual Scottish jokes about being tight flew around for a few days. But you don't take the mickey out of Gary too much. Both Alan and I recognise that he is a very good player and as we are all in direct competition as central defenders, Alan and I have developed a healthy respect for him.

Sammy Lee played his part in that double success and we were all very sad when he left for QPR, particularly because of the circumstances. For some reason the Anfield fans started to give him a bad time. If things were not going well on the pitch it was always Sammy who got the blame. And it all came to a head when he was substituted one day, and the crowd actually cheered when he was called off. It's so unlike the Liverpool fans, and I know it upset Sammy because he was one of them at heart. A Liverpudlian through and through, he worked his way up through the ranks to become a first-team player and an international. When the fans turned against him I think Sammy decided he had no alternative but to move on. Maybe it was because he was a local boy; it has happened to lots of other home-town players, but you don't expect it at Anfield.

He was a great favourite in the dressing room and nothing was too much trouble for him. We called him 'Quasi', which was a bit over the top, but he could take that kind of thing with a big smile on his face. Sammy had a wine bar in Liverpool and we were regular customers making sure that if we had an event organised we would take our custom there. He had some terrific characters as his friends. It was such a shame he had to leave because to wear the red shirt was all he ever wanted to do.

When Kevin MacDonald arrived I soon christened him 'Albert', after Albert Tatlock in *Coronation Street*, because he was always moaning. Some people are actually happy if they have something to beef about and Kevin was like that. It was not that he was the miserable type but it was his nature to look on the gloomy side and his introduction to the team didn't help. He came in when Graeme Souness left, but it was ridiculous to call him Graeme's replacement because nobody was going to step into his shoes, just as nobody can hope to replace Rushie.

Kevin is not the most elegant footballer around and the fans took a long time to recognise his value to the team. In fact it was only during the championship run-in that he began to get the credit he deserved. I have no doubt that he is one of the most influential players in the team when the chips are really down. He is not a spectacular player, but he does an essential job which really came through in those decisive final games. Just when he was becoming accepted by the public he had the misfortune to suffer a bad leg break at Southampton at the start of the following season.

Our paths had crossed earlier when he was at Leicester and I was with Brighton, so I knew from personal experience that he was a hardy player. He showed he had character as he battled to overcome those difficult days at the start of his Anfield career.

Inevitably, he was tagged by Alan Hansen before very long. We had a testimonial night arranged for Sammy Lee and the instructions were to wear a collar and tie. Kevin turned up in a pin-stripe suit which was not exactly the very latest in fashion. He had the misfortune to be on Alan's table and he immediately said 'Here's Louis. Where is your machine gun case?' After that it was 'Louis' MacDonald. Kevin's moaning also earned him the title 'Stroppy Joe' which soon became plain 'Stroppy'.

Paul Walsh is a bouncy little character who does not say a lot, but when he does he can be relied on for a few gems. Two glasses of lager are just about his limit in the alcohol stakes, then he is away. We named him 'Juice' because before one of his first games for Liverpool we were away in a hotel and at the pre-match meal he pointed to the orange drink and said 'Pass the juice'. That stuck with him until he became 'the Paraffin'. That stemmed from his way-out gear and his general appearance. Paul tried to grow a beard but it looked like something from a goat's chin, and with his long hair and strange clothes he got stuck with 'Paraffin Lamp', a play on tramp, which eventually became the Paraffin.

John Wark was also on the receiving end from Alan Hansen. When Jock Stein was the manager of Scotland, and Alan and John were in the squad for one game Jock said to John 'Am I right in thinking you are useless outside the penalty box?'. What he was trying to say was that John was such a prolific goal-scorer from mid-field he usually did all his damage inside the penalty area and that's where Jock wanted to see him play. But Norris made a note of that one and John had to take the stick when they returned to Anfield. John has played many times for Scotland and Alan insists that whenever he does they always get beaten. It's not true, of course, but it provides a bit more fun and banter. John was tagged 'Jinky' by Alan after another international. Jock asked him to play wide on the right and jink down the touchline which again is not exactly his strong point. It is fair to say he is our champion beer drinker. It doesn't matter how many he downs if we have a night out because it doesn't appear to have any effect on him whatsoever.

John could not drive when he arrived from Ipswich. I don't know if that is a Scottish quirk but it is surprising how many Scots do not drive. Steve Nicol was taking lessons when he arrived, and I know Graeme Sharp at Everton doesn't drive a car even now. It took Alan Hansen four attempts to pass his test – come to think of it, we should get some mileage out of that next time he slays one of us with one of his put downs, because even today Nigel Mansell he is most definitely not. Ronnie Whelan is not much better behind a wheel either. If he wants to reverse anywhere, no matter how much space is available, he insists on your getting out and guiding him in, and he only drives an Escort.

That was the squad, warts and all, which brought the double to Anfield.

HOW WE DID IT

Only Spurs and Arsenal had won the double this century before our name went into the Hall of Fame, the season after Heysel. It's not my style to boast but the more I think about it the more sure I am that there will never be another season quite like 1985–86 for a number of reasons. You cannot take anything away from the London clubs, but Liverpool's achievement will be remembered as something quite unique, and I wonder if the club received its due recognition beyond Merseyside for what it did.

When we began that season the shadow cast by Heysel was still very much a part of our lives. We had a new manager and nobody knew how he would cope, particularly as he was still an integral part of the team. We knew that the days of performing in Europe were a thing of the past for an indefinite period, and the after effects of what had happened left a deep scar.

Different players react in different ways. Bruce Grobbelaar spoke out in public of his serious doubts about continuing to play the game. Others also had misgivings although they kept their thoughts to themselves, but whichever way you look at it no team had ever prepared for a new campaign with such a heavy burden to carry.

There were our supporters to think about, too. Any success we have enjoyed has always been down to them in some degree because true to their anthem we have never walked alone. Many of them, however, were talking of turning their back on the game after Heysel, and we wondered if the famous Anfield atmosphere, which has lifted us so many times in the past was about to disappear. There is no ground like it on big occasions and the fans must have been as troubled as we were as the new season approached.

I was determined to carry on; I was a professional footballer before the Heysel disaster had happened and my argument was that in no way could the players be held responsible. We therefore had a duty to play our part in the re-birth of a stricken club.

The after effects of Heysel were intense. We all accepted that we would be under even greater scrutiny than ever before, both on and off the pitch, and that it was essential that we were seen to conduct ourselves correctly at all times. It was a matter of thinking before you said anything in case it was misinterpreted. Kenny Dalglish called us all together and stressed that, as we were in the firing line, the responsibility was ours to set the right example. It all conspired to bring us even closer together as a squad and Kenny's pre-season talk only reinforced that feeling. You never talk about winning things at Liverpool, certainly not in July, but without anything being said I think we all realised that there would never be a better chance to strike a blow for Liverpool Football Club, and to give the many thousands of innocent fans something good to remember after such a tragedy.

The whole build-up was different. For years Liverpool had a pre-season programme of matches played abroad, something which stemmed from the Bill Shankly era. He always favoured playing away from the home environment, claiming that matches against foreign opposition would not attract as much attention from the media if we lost. Results were secondary at this stage because the games were used as part of the fitness programme towards the new season. From Shankly's time onward it had become standard procedure, but this year Europe was closed to us even for friendly games and we were performing at such unlikely venues as Burnley, Bristol and Crewe. Even before a ball was kicked for real, our preparations had been drastically changed.

Those games were important because they were Kenny's settling in stage and by the time the season had started we all had a fair idea of what life was going to be like under the new manager. Taking orders from somebody who was a colleague a few months before did take some getting used to, and I'm sure the same applied to Kenny. There were never any of those uncomfortable moments when a silence descends as soon as the manager walks through the door, and I think Kenny appreciated that – we could sympathise with him in his new role, because if the heat was on for us, it was at boiling point for him.

Alan Hansen soon took over as captain that season from Phil Neal, which was a popular choice because Alan was a top quality player who had earned the respect of every member of the team. When the first League game came up we realised what was at stake. We were playing Arsenal at Anfield, and without doubt that was the most nerve-wracking game of my career. I've played in a few Cup finals, top European games and at international level, but I cannot recall a more tense occasion than our first game after Heysel. It seemed that the world's press was at Anfield that day, and no team has been subjected to such an intense glare of publicity. The pressure really affected me, and I wondered how Kenny was feeling for his first game in charge. We were all churning inside but if he felt the same way, he did not let on to any of us.

It's possible we won the championship on that first day because we played well enough to beat Arsenal. If it had all gone wrong on the pitch it's impossible to speculate what the effect would have been. But when the final whistle went we all instinctively felt we had cleared a massive hurdle in our minds. Really, we never looked back after that and I am sure it was the events at Anfield against Arsenal which set the tone for the duration of the season.

Even so it was different from any other year. Kenny would change the team around for certain games making it clear that he was going to do the job his way, and more often than not he was proved right. After years of doing it one way, however, it did come as a shock to the system when it became evident that what had happened before was now history, and that this was going to be Kenny Dalglish's Liverpool team performing the way he wanted us to perform regardless of what had been the norm before. The only thing that didn't change was the training. The tried and trusted methods which had become our trademark remained, so the regular sessions at Melwood were not altered, and if it was all change on match day at least we knew what we were doing for the remainder of the week.

One significant alteration was that Kenny decided we should all eat together at Anfield after training. This had been scrapped a few years earlier as an economy measure, but Kenny wanted everyone together after a morning session and did a deal with the cleaning ladies at the ground to provide some lunch in the players' lounge. It was accepted that the players would be expected to pay for this, but it was a good move, because instead of everybody drifting off home around midday it meant we stayed together a little longer and everybody, right down to the YTS lads and all the coaching and training staff, had a chance to talk and iron out any difficulties. It started just as sandwiches and tea but rapidly progressed to cooked meals, and today you can virtually choose the meal you want because the menu has become quite extensive.

There were other changes, too. We stayed in new hotels in different locations for away matches and the practice of not going down to Wembley for a Cup final until 24 hours before a game was scrapped, and we travelled on the Thursday, which is normal procedure for most clubs but never the Liverpool way until Kenny took over.

In the aftermath of Brussels, Crown Paints, the club's sponsors came up with the idea of the players presenting fans with autographed footballs before the kick-off, and made sure we covered all four sides of the ground. Crown Paints also started a Fan Club scheme designed to bring the players into closer contact with the supporters – a sensible move which helped to cement the link between us and the public at a time when it was essential that we all pulled together. On the surface these may have seemed unimportant moves, but they went a long way towards creating a bond which grew as the season progressed.

The early departure of Phil Neal and Alan Kennedy that season was another sign that the times were changing. Both had been a part of Liverpool's great days in Europe, but it was a signal to the rest of us that nothing lasts forever, particularly when a new young manager was in a hurry to restore the team to the very top. Phil had been my room mate ever since I joined the club so his departure meant a change in routine for me. Alan – 'Barney' to the fans, who had named him after a character in the Fred Flintstone series – had the rare distinction for a full back of having scored in two European Cup finals, and being on the winning side each time.

Things were going well in the League as the season progressed, but we never gave the FA Cup a thought until after Christmas, and the prospect of achieving the double never crossed our minds. The Cup affects players differently, however. When you wait for the third round draw to be made you are aware that it takes only half a dozen games to get to Wembley and that the draw is all important. Get a home game against anyone and you feel relieved, get an away game even against a team from a lower division, and that is something else.

We drew Norwich at home in the third round and the game was played in a snow storm. Nothing was going to stop us that day and we ran out 5–0 winners, ending a lean spell in the League in which we had played five games without a win. Even though we were at home, Kenny sprang another surprise by playing Jan Molby in a five man defence, but with a scoreline like that nobody was complaining.

That victory put us back on the rails in the League too. We had been gradually whittling away at Manchester United's lead at the top before a little stumble over Christmas, but after Norwich we had wins over Watford and West Ham, before our next big test in the Cup. Chelsea away was going to be difficult. They were doing well in the League, and Stamford Bridge had always been one of those grounds where we seemed to struggle, particularly in the FA Cup, as past results have proved.

This day was going to be different, however, because Chelsea lost Kerry Dixon in the opening minutes with a groin injury and Colin Lee was another casualty. Ian Rush had given us the lead in the first half, and I managed one of my rare goals before David Speedie pulled one back too late to affect the result. We were not the most popular team in West London that day. We played it tight and did not take any chances, and I don't suppose the television audience will remember it as one of the most riveting Cup ties of the season. But this was a very significant result and our Cup campaign was beginning to take shape.

Next came one of those potentially tricky clashes we would have preferred to avoid. York away may not sound too daunting, but they had a history of Cup upsets, and when we got there the pitch was rock hard and barely playable. Indeed, but for the presence of the television cameras it's doubtful whether the match would have started at all. We were happy to get away with a draw thanks to a Jan Molby penalty, but if we thought we had done the hard work we were in for a surprise when York came to Anfield. We needed extra time to get through. This was the only occasion throughout the Cup run when I thought we had blown it. It's history now, yet when the score was 1–1 York scored what I thought was a legitimate goal. Their big striker, Keith Walwyn, got between Gary Gillespie and Bruce Grobbelaar, and put the ball in the net. I was convinced it was a valid effort, and turned away to wait for the re-start before I realised that the referee had disallowed it, I don't know why. The destination of the FA Cup can depend on decisions like these.

The following Saturday, Everton beat us at Anfield in the League to emerge as the new favourites for the title, while they were still maintaining their own Cup run. We were aware of that but nobody could have foreseen what a dramatic climax we were both heading for at the end of the season. That derby defeat in February was highly significant because we did not lose another League game for the rest of the season.

In the sixth round we were paired with Watford at Anfield, and this was another game destined to go to a replay. Tony Coton, one of the most underrated keepers in the country, shut us out on that day, but an extra-time goal from Rushie put us through 2–1 at Vicarage Road.

We had made it to the semi finals and so had Everton. Only then did we start to speculate on the possibility of an all-Mersey final. Most of us did not believe it would ever happen because in the past whenever both clubs had reached the last four we always seemed to meet at the semi final stage, but not this year. Surely confirmation that it was destined to be the most memorable of all time, certainly for Merseyside. It was Everton v Sheffield Wednesday and Liverpool v Southampton.

There was more to come on a personal note. After we had beaten Watford we played Oxford in a League match and won it 6–0. Again I managed a goal, but I also suffered a stress leg fracture in a harmless looking collision with Peter Rhoades-Brown. It was to keep me out of the semi final and also to start a massive guessing game which was never given an answer. The only man who could supply it was Kenny Dalglish, I never asked and he never said. I realised that I would not be fit for the semi final and from past experience I knew the biggest problem for any Liverpool player was dropping out of the side through injury, because the hardest task of all at Anfield is regaining your place. Competition is always fierce and when the team is playing at top level, as it was by now, I certainly could not take anything for granted.

In the semi final that man Rush did it again with two extra-time goals to put us through to Wembley, and the final Merseyside had dreamed about for so many years. In the League we were neck and neck with Everton and the excitement was building up to fever pitch, which was marvellous for the fans but little consolation for me.

Gary Gillespie had taken my place and was performing with his usual calm and consistency. Gary has always been a very good player and he knew as well as I did just how high the stakes were now. Slowly my leg began to heal, but in the meantime Gary, who was no more a goal-scorer than I was, proceeded to produce a hat trick against Birmingham with Wembley just two weeks away. Great for Gary, a good friend of mine, but scant comfort for me. Before this season had ended we were all to discover that there is nothing certain in football, and that if you start taking things for granted you are sure to be proved wrong.

The week before Gary's hat trick Kenny had brought me back against West Brom, when Gary had a minor knock. I was not 100 per cent fit, but desperate to play as time was running out for me. I told Kenny how I felt and he selected me, but the following week Gary was back and I was on the sub's bench, a very disappointed man. The realisation that we would be playing Everton at Wembley, and that the championship race was strictly a two-horse event, brought home to us all the fact that there was everything to play for, not just for Liverpool but for Everton, too. One team could win the double, or we could win one trophy each. At that stage I don't think we would have been too upset if fate had decreed that we share the spoils, because the prospect of finishing empty-handed was just too awful to contemplate. 63

I'm sure the Everton lads felt the same way.

I had taken a chance on my fitness because I was needed at West Brom, and we had won, so to be out again so close to Wembley was a bitter pill to swallow. I have never believed I had a divine right to be in the team and would never dream of making a fuss, certainly not in public, if I was left out. We were on the brink of making history for the club, however, and the prospect of missing out at this late stage was hard to take. The crunch came in the League 10 days before Wembley. We were due at Leicester, while Everton was playing at Oxford on the same night. Again, I was the substitute as we won 2–0, and Everton surprisingly was beaten. So the scene was set for the final League game of the season. A win at Chelsea would wrap up the championship regardless of what Everton did in their final match at home to Southampton.

When we arrived in London on the Friday night, Jan Molby went down with a stomach upset. By Saturday morning he was worse and I was back in the side operating in a five man defence as sweeper. This was good news for me but then you always discover there is somebody worse off than yourself and in this instance it was Steve McMahon. He had been out of the side after injury but was fit and ready and knew this was his last chance to stake a claim for the Wembley team against his old club. The boss, however, decided to play me as the extra man in defence so Steve had to settle for the sub's role.

Stamford Bridge that day turned out to be a fairy tale. Who else could write a script which sees the player–manager score the championship-winning goal with a magnificent effort? We played well as a team on the day, and once that goal went in, it was easy for us and we could rightly claim to have won it in style. It was a glorious day but it ended with a strange twist. Our coach broke down on the way home and the replacement vehicle which picked us up outside Coventry happened to be Everton's official coach which was travelling south to London empty when it heard our SOS over the radio link. It still had Everton Football Club's sign on the windscreen when it pulled up to collect us. The irony of it was not lost on us; we had taken the championship from Everton, and now we had their bus, too.

From a personal point of view, I didn't know what the week would have in store. There was endless speculation from the press. Would Jan come back now he had recovered? Would I play, would Gary, and who would drop out? Typically, the manager said nothing and offered no clues as the big day approached. It certainly helped to keep us all on our toes if nothing else, but to me and the other players involved it was more like a Scottish variation of the Chinese water torture. We knew he would not name the team until we reached our Wembley dressing room so the game of patience was going to be played to the end. But, as fate would have it, Gary Gillespie went down sick.

We had travelled down on the Thursday to our Watford hotel and everybody trained as normal. I put Gary's problem down to Wembley nerves, and was quite sure he would shake it off before the team was announced. But, on the Saturday morning, we realised it was more serious than that because Gary had to take a fitness test.

When he returned we were told he was not fit and it went through my mind that now I had a real chance of being selected – and that is what happened, with Steve McMahon chosen as sub. A lot was made of the fact that not only were there no local lads in our team, but there were no Englishmen in our ranks either. I modified that into a good quiz question; 'Who was the only English-born player in Liverpool's 1986 Cup final team?'. It caught a few people out because although I was from Preston most people thought I was Irish because of my international career. They could have linked me with anywhere under the sun that day because I was just so happy and relieved to be in the team. I could fully sympathise with Gary, and one of the nicest gestures at the end of the game was when the Liverpool fans chanted his name just to let him know he had not been forgotten. That's typical of what happens with our fans. In or out of the team they let you know you are still part of the set up.

The fans of both sides did themselves proud; Liverpool and Everton had faced each other in the Milk Cup final but this was the big one and the fans sensed it too. Everyone was on their best behaviour which was the perfect adver-tisement for Merseyside. The humour that has always been the area's trademark was there for all to see, and the atmosphere must have made a lasting impression all over the world, as the game was seen live on television. Coming 12 months after Heysel I'm sure the Scouse fans at Wembley, red and blue, went a long way to restoring the battered image of the region and its football followers by the way they conducted themselves on that day.

As for the game, we were never really in it in the first half. Gary Lineker put Everton in front and after a promising start, no matter how we tried, we just could not get it together. The half-time talk was simple and succinct; this game was there to be won, and really there was no more to be said.

We had a few more scares early in the second half. Bruce and Jim Beglin got into a tangle and angry words were exchanged, although for the life of me I can't believe they could understand each other; you try listening to an excited South African and a lad from deepest Ireland. After that, we needed one of Bruce's extra-special saves to tip over a Graeme Sharp header, and I think that was the turning point. I don't think any other keeper could have kept that one out. He was well off his line, but being the supreme athlete he is he somehow still got to it. It must have demoralised Everton because they were never the same again, while we seemed to move up a gear.

When Rushie scored the equaliser, Everton were beginning to look tired and it must have flashed through their minds that we had never lost a game when Rushie had scored. I can't say I thought about it at the time because I was so wrapped up in the game, but we were looking the stronger side at that stage, and when you believe you are going to win it takes a lot to shake you out of your stride.

Craig Johnston put us in front before Rushie struck again, and the double was in the bag. But even as we collected our winners' medals and took off on our lap of honour, the full significance had not sunk in. The championship was one thing, but the double! That takes an awful lot of digesting and it was several days before I was able to absorb it all. All my misgivings earlier in Cup final week had disappeared, but when I look back on the events it's impossible to say what I might have done if I had missed that Cup final. The manager picks the team, you either go along with that or not, and I have always been the type to accept decisions whether I agreed with them or not. I admit that if I had been left out of the Cup final it would have been a shattering blow, definitely my worst experience since becoming a Liverpool player. But we shall never know what was in Kenny's mind that week. He certainly never offered any clues as to what he was thinking, and why should he? The problem of choosing between Gary and me never arose in the end although it is human nature to wonder just what he would have done if Gary had been available.

Perhaps there is a lesson there for other managers. If Kenny had named his team on Friday and been forced to change it the next day, what effect would that have had on the players concerned? Kenny avoided any personality clashes before the big game because he is a cautious man by nature, but I would not call him lucky because he didn't have to make the decision; the luck was all against Gary Gillespie on the day.

I'm not suggesting that Kenny dodged the issue, because that is not his style. All through the season, we had come to realise that team changes, new tactics and new formations were always going to be a part of his style of management. We don't have any so-called stars at Liverpool, as far as the management is concerned; even Kenny had been left out of the side by Joe Fagan after a Cup tie against Stockport. I remember he took that decision quietly, with the minimum of fuss. If a player of his calibre can accept being left out why shouldn't lesser mortals like myself? But at the time I could not have guaranteed to have approached it with such a philosophical attitude.

Looking back on that season, we had surpassed anything in our wildest dreams and, apart from one isolated incident where a few of the Manchester United players had been victims of a spray gun attack when they arrived at Anfield, there had been no unsavoury incidents. The crowd's behaviour had been excellent, and we all thought we had completed a job in a way we had reason to be proud of. It was a very important season for Liverpool Football Club and it ended in an unprecedented fashion.

THE MANAGERS

If you must be mad to be a manager, put me down for the funny farm. I have worked for all sorts and the longer I have been in the game the more I fancy a crack at managing. That's why I applied for the Republic job, and when the time comes I shall devote as much thought and preparation applying for a club appointment as I did when I wrote to Dublin.

Because the turnover in managers is so great I have played for many people of vastly different temperaments. Extraverts, introverts, ranters and ravers, bully boys, sergeant majors, you name them, I've met them. What it has taught me is that it takes a very complex person to become a successful manager.

Perhaps more significantly I have come to realise that being a good player doesn't automatically make you a good manager. If that were the case the top managers in the game today would certainly include the names of Bobby Charlton, Bobby Moore, Denis Law, George Best and a few more of the all-time greats. The reverse, however, seems to be the case. In my time in the game the top managers have been men like Bob Paisley, Joe Fagan, Harry Catterick, Bertie Mee, and more recently Dave Bassett, Graham Taylor and Howard Kendall. They could all play but none of them were internationals, yet as managers they have earned the respect and admiration of football fans throughout the country for their achievements.

The first professional manager I came into contact with was Alan Ball senior, who was in charge at Preston when I was a schoolboy player. I did not have a lot to do with him simply because at the age of 14 I was just one of many hopeful youngsters starting out in the game. He still made quite an impression on me, however. Alan knew the names of every member of staff, including the schoolboys, and when a League manager takes the time to spend a few minutes with you whenever he meets you, and knows your name, it goes a long way towards making you feel part of the establishment, even at such a young age. He liked to get everyone around him to talk football and made sure nobody was left out.

Arthur Cox was his trainer and they were a good combination, particularly in their early days at Preston. The side was successful and going for promotion one Christmas, but even when it all collapsed in the second half of the season and Preston were almost relegated Alan kept the same players in the team. In the end, that decision cost Alan his job because he remained too loyal to his players when anyone else could see it was going wrong. Lesson number one for probationary manager Lawrenson.

Alan brought a character from Halifax with him to Deepdale. Harry Hubbick, who is still around today, was the original Bolton full back; he's tough, battle-scarred, and has a nose which looks as if it's the result of going 15 rounds with Henry Cooper, for seven days non-stop. Bolton was the real hard nut of football at one time, and looking at Harry's face it is easy to understand why. He always liked players who were prepared to put their foot in, no doubt reminding him of the good old days when he did the same thing at Burnden Park.

Alan told a lovely tale about Harry when they were at Halifax. They did not train at the Shay so Harry was always the last to leave the ground after attending to any injured players, and the first to set off in order to brew the tea. Harry was very proud of his motor car; he was the type who would wash it religiously three times a week so that it was always spick and span, and in the winter he would even put a blanket over the radiator to make sure the pipes did not crack. He was meticulous in every detail, and also an extremely careful driver.

This particular day he was on his way to the Shay in his new MG 1100, his latest pride and joy. The traffic was heavy both ways so Harry was crawling along taking no chances. His caution was so extreme that the person behind him could not get past despite several abortive attempts. When Harry approached the Shay and the right hand turn in to the ground, the traffic had eased and the impatient driver behind him decided to overtake. At exactly the same moment Harry swung into the middle of the road, and there was

69

the inevitable collision. Out jumped the irate motorist to harangue Harry about his lack of signals and excessively slow driving. Poor Harry hadn't a leg to stand on, and all he could think to say was 'You should have known I was going into the football ground, because I'm wearing a track-suit'. How the poor man was supposed to have known that before Harry got out of his car is a mystery, but it was all Harry could think of to say. Perhaps if the guy had realised how Harry worshipped his car he might have been a little more sympathetic.

When 'Bally' left and Harry Catterick eventually took over at Preston there was quite a stir in the media. Here was a man who had won the Cup and the championship for Everton, and now he was going to put Preston back on the map. There was a weekly television show devoted to soccer in the North West in those days called *Kick Off*, bringing all the latest news of clubs in the area and they sent a camera crew to Deepdale to spend a day watching Harry at work.

That type of thing came easily to him because he had been in the spotlight at Everton. The cameras filmed interviews, and the players at work, before Harry took them on a con-ducted tour of the ground. Harry knew all the right things to say and everything was progressing smoothly until they arrived at the treatment room where Harry Hubbick was attending to a player.

In swept the manager followed by the camera crew and the interviewer, and Harry grandly introduced Preston's team physiotherapist to the watching millions. That's when it all went wrong – Catterick asked Harry to speak. 'What's this lad's problem?' asked the manager. Harry, who was working busily on the treatment table, turned around, saw all the lights and cameras and promptly froze. 'He's got a knee, boss', was all he could manage. The cameras kept rolling for a few more seconds before the producer realised there were no more words coming and ordered, 'Cut'. In football parlance everyone knew what Harry meant but to the viewing public it seemed as though he was just stating the obvious, because the poor lad was stretched out with his knee as the focus of attention. For the next few days poor Harry led a dog's life thanks to the rest of us. We were forever knocking on his door and saying 'Harry, I've got a knee', or an ankle, or just about anything.

The same guy perfected the art of grabbing 40 winks at the slightest opportunity. I have never known anyone drop off so quickly. On away trips the bus would be barely out of the grounds before Harry was off, with his mouth open, catching flies. Roy Tunks and Mike Elwiss were the practical jokers at Preston in those days and they decided to stitch up Harry once and for all. As soon as Harry had dozed off they tied both his feet together and strapped him into his seat by the waist and throat. Mike then crept up behind him and clapped his hands as loudly as possible. It sounded like a gun going off and Harry promptly shot forward and nearly strangled himself.

You can pull stunts like that only on people you genuinely like and I'm sure the lads at Preston today who bump into him will know what I mean. Football clubs are not just about big personalities or star players. The real characters in the game are the unsung heroes like Harry who have dedicated themselves to football all their lives and are prepared to do any job for the benefit of the club. Without the Harry Hubbicks of this world the game would be the poorer.

Bobby Charlton, who took over from Alan Ball, was the only manager I have encountered who did not seem to enjoy the job. I'm sure you need a mean streak to succeed – lesson number two for me – and Bobby just did not have it. That was not his fault; we are all made differently and Bobby, a player I idolised as a kid, just could not handle the inevitable hassle that goes with management. He didn't like players knocking on his door and asking why they had been left out of the team and instead of telling them to clear off he would feel guilty about dropping them.

He was kind to a fault. When he arrived he brought former Manchester United players with him, and Nobby Stiles, David Sadler and Francis Burns all did a good job for the team. When it was going smoothly Bobby was happy, but when it came to making potentially unpopular decisions he found it difficult. I can understand that; as a player it had been success all the way for him and he came to Deepdale as player–manager.

Turning out at places like Colchester and Halifax must

have been a shock to his system after all the glory with England and United. Invariably the Third Division teams would put two men on him just to stop him playing, which was a sad way for one of the great players to end his career. In training you could only marvel at his ability despite his advancing years. Nobody could take the ball from him and we would just gape with wonder as he fired in blinding 30-yard shots with either foot, seemingly without any effort. Even then he had all the skill in the world, but other Third Division managers were so afraid of him they just set out to stop him by any means. Bobby is one of the game's nice guys, but that can be a handicap in the tough world of management. I'm sure he was glad to bow out when he did and he has certainly shown no inclination to come back.

Bobby signed me as a professional and all the youngsters at the club wanted to be in his company as often as possible. When the weather was bad and the pitches unfit for training we used to work out at Kirkham Prison. Some of the first team had cars, but the young lads like myself would fight to get a lift from Bobby in his Range Rover, and it was commonplace to see as many as 10 of us scrambling to get aboard just to be with the boss. He was always happy to go along with that because I think he felt more comfortable working with the kids rather than facing the aggravation you get dealing with senior players.

Now he is a director of Manchester United and I'm sure that is more to his taste. As one of the finest ambassadors of the English game he was never cut out for the more basic life of running a Third Division club. That's another lesson for me, reinforced by Phil Neal's experience at Bolton.

If I am ever fortunate enough to get a player–manager's job I hope it will be with one of the top clubs because lower down everything is against you. Phil spent 10 great years at Liverpool before going to Bolton where there was no cash available, low gates and a permanent struggle to make ends meet. It really is a different world, as he discovered. He had some idea, of course, because he started out at Northampton, but after the Liverpool experience it must have been tough making the readjustment.

One of my old pals from Brighton, Brian Horton, has warned me of the dangers too. He became player–manager of Hull and I have kept in touch with him and watched his team on a number of occasions. He has stressed how demanding and how difficult the job can be, and I believe it will get worse.

Standards are dropping and it won't be long before the Fourth Division will have to go part-time and maybe the Third will too. That will mean fewer vacancies for full-time managers and I am realistic enough to accept that what I want may not be possible. At this stage, however, I have not thought beyond a career in management or coaching. I'm sure there is still tremendous satisfaction from working with youngsters, particularly if you can see some of them making the grade. I know management is a minefield but it doesn't stop me from believing that I have something to offer and from wanting to put into practice what I have learnt from so many different people.

Nobby Stiles, who also had a spell as manager of Preston after I had moved on, was in effect second-team boss when I was just starting out. Despite his image as an aggressive cantankerous individual on the field, he never shouted or yelled when he looked after the Preston lads. We were regularly beaten in the Central League because we were one of the youngest teams, but Nobby had the gift of gentle persuasion and if you were giving 100 per cent he was prepared to forgive the odd mistake. Nobby never asked you to do anything he could not do himself. Nothing was too much trouble for him – another important lesson to digest.

He lived in Manchester, and Deepdale was only five minutes away from the M6, but if any lad needed a lift to the railway station after training, Nobby could always be relied upon to volunteer even though it was going out of his way, and would put an extra half hour on his journey home.

I'm sure there will always be a position in football for Nobby because he is so popular with everyone who meets him. A genuine, sincere man, he is always ready to help and almost embarrassed by his great reputation in the game. That is another lesson, the art of modesty, which seems to come naturally to the people who have won the highest honours in the game.

Harry Catterick, who succeeded Bobby Charlton at Preston, was as different from him as chalk is from cheese.

He came with the reputation for being a stern disciplinarian who did not care who you were and what you might have done in the past. Everybody started equal with him before they were downgraded! Harry could walk down the corridor saying hello to three or four players and ignoring eight or nine – that was his way. You tended to be wary of him, and in some cases a little afraid, because he often kept his thoughts to himself and you were never quite sure what the next step would be. Maybe I was one of the favoured few because I never had any trouble with him. He always picked me for his team and I found him approachable although I know that was not the view shared by the majority of players at Preston during his time.

Anyone with an ego or an inflated opinion of themselves was asking for trouble with Harry. He was just not impressed, and from the first day he made it clear it would be done his way or else. He had no problem dropping players, regardless of who they were. If he felt you were not worth a place, that was it – finished. There was another lesson to be learnt, because when it came to strength of character you would be hard pressed to find anyone to match him, whether you thought he was right or wrong.

When I was transferred to Brighton, Harry wrote me a letter which I have kept; it showed the other side of someone who was supposed to be difficult to get on with. He told me that if I continued the way I had started at Preston there was no reason why I should not make it to a top club and enjoy a successful career. But if I had any problems along the way I should not hesitate to get in touch and he would be happy to advise me – so much for the moody introvert. I really appreciated that gesture and have not forgotten it.

I was told a story about Harry being continually upstaged by Bill Shankly when they were rivals on Merseyside, which underlined his problems of communication. It's doubtful whether anybody could compete with 'Shanks' when it came to public relations, and certainly not Harry. One day, tired of the comparisons, he apparently snapped and said 'It's not my fault that I don't speak like Rob Roy'. I can understand how he felt. We are all made differently and if you are naturally withdrawn it's virtually impossible to change your personality, especially when you are in the public eye, because attempting to fool people will soon expose you as an imposter.

Another manager I remember with respect is Arthur Cox, who is now regarded as one of the top managers after bringing Newcastle and Derby back to the First Division. He has kept in touch with me since I was a 14 year old at Preston. To an outsider, Arthur comes across as a rather distant figure, reluctant to appear on television or have his views quoted in the newspapers, but he is a caring person and is totally committed to football.

Alan Mullery, my boss when I joined Brighton, certainly had no problems putting himself across either in public or in the dressing room. The wonder is that he never burst a blood vessel because I've never known anyone lose his temper so often. That was his nature, but I picked something up from him, too. If you rant and rave every time things go wrong the force of your words tends to become devalued, and in the end players stop listening because they have heard it all before. Alan blew his top more often than Vesuvius. Again, in fairness, it was rarely directed towards me, but Alan just could not keep his mouth shut. Many a time we would pick up the newspapers to see him quoted as saying a certain player would never be in the Brighton team again, when he had not got round to saying so in the dressing room.

Alan didn't care who he was talking to, if he was boiling up it would all come out, whether to a player or a journalist. There was never a dull moment but there were occasions when Alan might have been better advised to count to 10 before letting off steam. I'm not sure that such a fiery temperament is the best for dealing with footballers. You can lay down the law but there are limits. If this sounds like an anti-Mullery tirade I'm conveying the wrong impression because he did a lot for me. He paid a record price of £110,000 to take me to Brighton, deflected all criticism about the size of that fee, and told me he would handle all that. The fact that I was taking the place of Graham Cross did not go down too well in some quarters, but again Alan backed me to the hilt, and Graham went in the opposite direction to Preston.

At first, the press kept describing me as, 'Record buy Mark Lawrenson' which could have been a burden, but eventually they dropped that tag and just let me get on with my game.

I knew Alan was defending me while I settled in and I appreciated that. The thing about Alan was that he would fight for you with everything he had if he was sure you were doing the same for him.

Nobody really had an argument with him because the conversation was always one way; he was right as far as he was concerned and that was the end of it. We were often tempted to pipe up, because he liked to call team meetings on a regular basis, but we soon realised it was not worth it. The meetings were designed for Alan to talk *at* us and he was not interested in what we may have been thinking.

One meeting stands out. It was during my last year at Brighton and we were struggling to avoid relegation. We had lost at home to Bristol City and there were only three or four games left to play. The position looked pretty desperate, so Alan called yet another meeting of all the players, with chairman Mike Bamber and another director present. I have never seen him so angry. He went through all the players individually saying how we had let the club and the town down, and then he said, 'You are all going to get me the sack'. He then turned to the chairman and added 'This man will sack me because of you lot, and I'll guarantee one thing. If I do get the sack and I see any of you walking down the street, I'll run you over.' The chairman remained silent, but Alan left at the end of that season.

That outburst was typical of Alan getting carried away and it happened so often. At half-time, if we were struggling, he would charge into the dressing room and give us all another burst of abuse, while he had his cup of tea. At the end of it he would be so wound up that the next step would be to hurl the cup against the wall simply because he was not prepared to let it go with words alone. That was always the signal for everyone to duck and to get back onto the pitch as quickly as possible, because the action was often less fraught out there than it was in the dressing room.

He was a bit of a Jekyll and Hyde. He loved a beer with the boys when things were going right and could be the life and soul of the party. In retrospect I'm not sure that was such a good idea either, because if you want to play the tyrant one day and be one of the lads the next it does put your credibility in some doubt. I liked him because I knew the rages and frustration all stemmed from his desire to do well and from his sheer enthusiasm for Brighton. He was also prepared to support me. He was one of those people who took it as a personal affront if we were ever beaten. Perhaps this was the old business of a keen committed player, as he was, trying to relive his playing career through the men he now controlled.

You could not fault his knowledge of the game and until that fateful last season he had a very good record of results with Brighton. He was a strict disciplinarian and fines were commonplace if you were late for training. You faced more fines if you were booked or sent off, and if he agreed with the referee's decision.

As a player he had been powerful and fearless and he used these qualities on occasions as a manager. If anyone was struggling to get fit for a game he would join them in the treatment room and remind them of the number of times he had turned out for Spurs and Fulham when he was not 100 per cent fit if he felt his presence on the field would help his team. That kind of talk would influence you.

His pre-match talks were quite an education, too, and I'm told by players who worked for the great Bill Shankly that he often took the same line. Alan was always running down the opposition. Before we played Nottingham Forest in a Cup tie, he wrote all their names on a blackboard and then proceeded to criticise each one. He did this even though they were a good side in those days, rivalling Liverpool as the best around. Alan wrote down the names of Peter Shilton, Larry Lloyd, John Robertson, Tony Woodcock, Viv Anderson and Garry Birtles and then dismissed them saying 'They are has-beens. If you lot can't beat them I may as well pack it in.'

It may sound artificial but it worked. He would build our confidence sky-high so we really believed we were going to win every time we went out – at least on the good days. He certainly boosted my confidence and I never needed an agent to look after my affairs because Alan was forever extolling my virtues. Ah, what it is to be one of the favoured few! It certainly didn't do my prospects any harm and he did as much as anyone for me in my four years with Brighton.

The famous Mullery temper had a field day when we

returned from a disastrous mid-season break to Jersey. It was Alan's idea to send us there because we were preparing for a 'promotion push', and the signs were looking good. It was my second season with the club and when a trip to the Channel Islands, with no training involved, was suggested we were all naturally in favour.

We beat Leicester on the Saturday and were due to fly out the next morning for a four day break, but at the last moment Alan had to pull out, so his assistant Ken Craggs was to be the man in charge. Ken was a real character; I think he had been a tailor in London before he teamed up with Alan. He never had a cigarette out of his mouth and he was a keen follower of the horses. He was very popular with the lads and although nobody mentioned it at the time most of the boys were more than happy to have Ken in charge, rather than Alan.

We all assembled at the ground on Sunday morning for the short drive to Gatwick, but the weather was miserable when we arrived at the airport for what is only a quick flight and we were told it was delayed because of the fog. We all went straight into the bar for a few drinks; after all, this was a break with no work involved and there was nothing else to do until the flight was called. We had been told we were going there to enjoy ourselves so what harm was there in a couple of beers before we set off?

When we eventually did get away we had a bumpy ride to Jersey and a few more drinks, just to settle the nerves of course! On arrival we were met by some local club officials who invited us into the airport bar for a couple of pints. By this time we didn't require a second invitation. We had a players' kitty with us of around £300, the result of small fines for penalties imposed for minor irregularities. Ken had told us that all our food would be free, but if we wanted any alcohol we would have to pay for it ourselves. Here we were, in Jersey, back at the bar, already feeling 'in the spirit of things' and our kitty so far untouched.

When we reached our hotel we headed for the restaurant to have something to eat and decided to open the kitty because we were all in the mood by now. Within two hours the kitty was a thing of the past. I felt a nap was called for and disappeared to my room to sleep off the effects; within an hour my telephone was ringing and Ken Craggs was ordering me to his room in the next 10 minutes. When I arrived most of the boys were sitting around and there was a strange silence. Ken did not look happy either and I wondered what was going on.

Brian Horton was standing behind Ken trying to attract my attention but I could not imagine why. Looking around I noticed our goalkeeper, Graham Moseley, was missing and realised that something must have happened. The door opened and in walked Graham with his hand heavily strapped. Then Ken started. 'What did I tell you? By all means enjoy yourselves, but don't go crazy. Look what has happened. Graham has put his hand through a plate-glass window and I've got to ring the boss and tell him he won't be fit to play for two or three weeks because he has had stitches. And this has all happened within hours of us arriving.'

We were all sobering up pretty fast now when he added 'But there is worse. I've just had the hotel manager on the phone saying that somebody has thrown up in reception. Who is going to own up to that? You might as well tell me now because I will find out eventually.' There was silence, so Ken tried again. 'Whoever it was, just say so, because I am going to have to sort it out with the hotel.'

Kenny Tiler, the full back turned to Graham and said 'Are you going to tell him or shall I?'. Poor Graham said 'Tell him what? It wasn't me, I swear it.' But Kenny Tiler gave him a hard stare and Graham capitulated. 'OK Ken, it was me', he admitted. Just then there was a knock at the door from the hotel manager. He was ushered in, received an apology from Graham and agreed that nothing more would be said about the incident.

Ken Craggs, anticipating what Alan Mullery's response would be, concocted a tale to protect Graham, saying he had had an accident and his hand had gone through a window which was obviously weak. He would skirt around the throwing up incident. Surprisingly, Mullery received the message with relative calm, much to the relief of a very worried Ken. He once again emphasised the need to stay in line and not to do anything else which might cause trouble. After that he had a roll call every morning just to check what kind of shape we were in, and the rest of the trip passed off uneventfully until the morning we were due to return to Brighton.

Alan Mullery rang early to tell Ken that three of the players, Graham Winstanley, John Ruggiero and Eric Potts, were needed for a reserve team game that night against Charlton. So there was no more boozing for that trio. We were checking out of the hotel at 9.30 am for the flight back home when the message came through that the airport was closed because of fog, and that they had no idea when it would be possible to take off. Ken rang Alan to tell him the news, but by then our manager was not a happy man. Obviously the news of Graham's injury must have sunk in. He put Ken right on the spot telling him to get us off the island somehow or other. Short of ordering us to swim, there was nothing Ken could do about it.

The delay was indefinite so, apart from the three lads due to play that night, we had time for a few more drinks both at the hotel and the airport. The flight was so late that we did not make Gatwick until 5 pm and waiting for us was a furious Alan Mullery. He had driven up from Brighton and had obviously been hanging around for an awfully long time. He had a half eaten cigar in his mouth and we all knew what to expect because we had seen it all before. Poor Ken Craggs was the first victim.

'What time do you call this?' he bellowed. What could Ken say? It was not his fault the flights were delayed, but the boss was fuming now because of the reserve game. He turned to our coach driver and pinned him against the side of the bus ordering him to get the lads to the ground in 30 minutes, which was a pretty tall order from Gatwick. He put the fear of God into the hapless driver who assured him he would do his best.

Alan was so angry that he forgot the obvious solution which was to take the three players back in his Jaguar. Instead, he disappeared with Ken, leaving George Aitken to get the rest of us to the Goldstone in the bus. Within minutes of setting off the coach broke down on the M23. We could see the funny side of it and the three due to play were being offered more drinks because it seemed impossible for them to get back in time for the match. As luck would have it, in a very short time an empty coach belonging to the same company rolled up, and we were hastily transferred onto that. By the time we had got there the game had started with Brighton down to just eight men.

Harry Cripps, an ex-player, was in charge of the Charlton side. He was another real London character, and had refused our manager's request for the kick-off to be put back, because he obviously sensed that there was a problem. One way and another our gaffer was in a hell of a mood by now, and we were determined to watch the fun. We filed into the grandstand to witness the fireworks, and we were not disappointed. It was known that Alan and Harry did not see eye to eye at the best of times so this promised to be something special.

The three lads who were due to play disappeared into the dressing room for a quick change while we took our seats. It was a 'no win' situation for them, as our boss was screaming and shouting in the dug out at anyone and everyone who came within earshot. It did not take long before Harry Cripps was involved, too, and at one stage the two of them squared up to each other. At this point Graham Winstanley came down the tunnel and was waiting by the touchline to go on, knowing we were all rocking with laughter in the gods, at the best pantomime show staged at Brighton for years. Inevitably, Brighton lost and a mid-season break was never suggested again. Ken Craggs was never left in charge of us again either, which was rough on him because he could not be blamed for what happened.

After Brighton and Mullery there could be no greater contrast than Liverpool and Bob Paisley. Here was a man who had won everything and who enjoyed a world-wide reputation, which put him on the same level as those legendary figures Matt Busby, Jock Stein and Bill Shankly. I admit I was a little apprehensive when I went with my stepfather to meet him for the first time. How do you approach a man of his stature? It was not the same as meeting Bobby Charlton for the first time as a teenager. I admired Charlton for his qualities as a player, but Paisley had a record which no one could challenge as the manager of the top club in the country.

He was different all right. To be honest, when he opened

the conversation I could not understand what he was talking about, and I just hoped my stepfather was getting the gist of it. If you put Bob Paisley on *What's My Line*, blindfolded the panel, and managed to disguise his distinctive voice nobody would ever, repeat ever, guess he was a football manager. A less likely looking one you could never meet. He is more like everyone's favourite grandfather. He is quiet, almost shy, makes a mockery of the popular image that a successful manager must be trendy and outspoken. Everything you associate with success goes out of the window when you meet Bob Paisley for the first time. But who got it right, and who got it wrong?

Even after I had signed and been at Anfield for a while I just could not believe this was the man guiding Liverpool. His appearance and demeanour just did not tally with my idea of a top soccer boss. We saw him every day although he didn't take an active role in the training, that was in the hands of Joe Fagan and Ronnie Moran. It was only when I started to work for the man that I began to realise what he was all about. It's accepted throughout the game that his knowledge of football is outstanding, and on medical matters he is in a class of his own. He had qualified as a physiotherapist years before and his ability to diagnose injuries is a byword in the game.

Apparently, before one match against Derby he had turned to Tommy Docherty, who was their manager at the time, and told him Charlie George had a knee problem, just on the evidence of watching Charlie at the kick-in. Tommy told him he knew nothing about an injury, but in a matter of weeks Charlie was having a cartilage operation. The same thing happened with Trevor Francis. Bob spotted something in the way Trevor was moving and forecast imminent surgery and was proved right again, long before Trevor's club had any idea that anything was wrong.

Stories abound about Bill Shankly; everybody who came into contact with him has a tale to tell, and he will never be forgotten. Bob Paisley came from the same school and although he is a totally different kind of person he is another man whom nobody will forget, least of all at Anfield. He rarely raised his voice and if he wanted to chide you he usually did it in the press. He understood that every player likes good publicity but hates criticism in public, and Bob would do it in such a way that it was never considered to be over the top, but he was getting his message across.

Playing for him was a totally new experience. Everything seemed to go like clockwork at Liverpool, as though nobody was in charge. That's the sign of success and the reason why it was such a well-administered club. Team meetings were another thing. We hardly had any. Bob never paid much attention to the opposition. If anybody had brought a blackboard or a video into a meeting we would have thought they had taken leave of their senses. Bob would call us together on a Friday morning and usually just say 'The same team as last week', and we would get on with it. He certainly didn't worry about who we were playing and that confidence got through to us without anything being said.

He always remembered what we had done in a game rather than how the opposition had shaped up. After we had played Arsenal on one occasion and won well at Highbury, Jimmy Hill spotlighted on television how Alan Hansen and I liked to play football from the back. He illustrated the point showing me on film coming forward and taking the ball past Lee Chapman. It all looked very effective, but the following week Bob took me to one side and said 'Don't forget, everybody in the First Division will have seen that on television and taken note of it'.

In my first season at Liverpool the rare team meetings were usually for the benefit of Bruce Grobbelaar. It was his first season, too, and inevitably he made some mistakes, the price of inexperience. Bob would get us together to help Bruce as much as anything. Bruce was trying too hard after taking over from Ray Clemence, and Bob was aware of this. He told Bruce that he would be quite happy with him if he did nothing in the game apart from take goal kicks. The point was that Bruce had been caught out on a couple of occasions coming for crosses he had no right to reach, but he was doing this to justify his place in the team. Bob told him he would be paid the same money if he stayed on his line and did nothing. It was his way of telling Bruce he did not have to prove that he was a good goalkeeper, because everyone at the club already knew that, not least Bob, who had bought him.

Bob would walk around Anfield in his slippers and an old cardigan, oblivious to anything people might think, but I'm sure many of the fans were puzzled by this ordinary looking man who had achieved so much for the club. When he left at the end of the day he would put on his coat and flat cap, and walk quietly to his car, with the minimum of fuss. I once read a remark which summed him up perfectly. When he retired as manager he was asked if he had any unfulfilled ambitions. 'Yes', he replied, 'to walk down the street and not be recognised.'

We were all the same in his eyes, regardless of who we were or how much we had cost. He was so down to earth, and there must be a lesson to be learnt from that, too. I don't know how anyone who has achieved as much as he has could remain so modest and serene throughout it all. To this day I have never seen him lose his temper, and he is still actively involved. As Kenny's consultant for two years he had his say at half-time in every match, and clearly still had a lot to offer the club. His secret was to know all his players and their quirks, and the experience of nearly 50 years with the club gave him a unique insight into how to run a club like Liverpool. Who could argue with his record?

When Joe Fagan took the chair he kept things ticking over very much in the Paisley style. He was a different type of person, always ready for a chat about anything under the sun; this bubbly character did not look his age in his first season, but looked considerably older in his second. Something happened to Joe in that second season, and it happened long before the Heysel disaster. I think he just got tired of the job and of the daily routine, and was happy to get out. Certainly, he is more like himself these days, and has started showing up at Anfield again after a long absence. Joe was a happy man, but he could be hard too; he only needed to show this hard streak twice to get his message across.

The first time was when he was still chief coach and we had lost 3–1 at home to Manchester City. Joe really hit the roof after that one – Alan Mullery would have been impressed. Even the top players in the side such as Kenny Dalglish, Graeme Souness and Ray Kennedy were silent as he read the riot act.

Joe's other outburst was more restrained but equally effective. When he became manager, Ronnie Moran took the training with Roy Evans, but on this particular day Ronnie was away at a funeral so Joe was back on the training ground with us. We were doing simple exercises involving two players at a time who were required to pass the ball to each other from a distance of 20 yards. Terry McDermott and Phil Thompson were the two involved, and typical of Terry who was always up to something, he drove the ball much too hard at Phil. It didn't matter because Phil managed to control it well but decided to give Terry one back in similar fashion. This one, however, flew off wildly, disrupting the exercise. Tommo started laughing – it was just a prank with Terry – but Joe was not amused. 'Don't ever take the mickey out of me again', was all he said in a very flat tone. That was the end of it, but the remainder of the session was conducted in silence because there was no mistaking the anger in Joe's voice.

To give you some idea of Joe's standing at the club, I think Graeme Souness had his best-ever season for Liverpool when Joe took over. We won three trophies and Graeme played with an inspired skill. He recognised that Joe was somebody special, to be treated with respect, and while that applied to the rest of us as well, Graeme was prepared to go out on the pitch and die for Joe. Bob Paisley had made him captain during his time and I think Graeme felt he had something to demonstrate to Joe when he became manager. Call it loyalty or commitment, but whatever it was Graeme was determined to help Joe in every possible way in his first season in charge.

Joe changed in the second season. I hope that he didn't have a premonition of the terrible events which were to come at Heysel, but certainly he was not the same man. He started to look old, and age was something you never associated with him, even though we all knew he was older than either Bill Shankly or Bob Paisley when he had become manager. In fact Bill was younger than Joe when he retired as manager. The enjoyment seemed to have gone out of the job in the second year.

The famous Anfield bootroom was always Joe's second home and he didn't change that when he took charge. It was 85 there that he spent his happiest times and he liked nothing better than to chew the fat with the rest of the backroom staff in that little room. Joe was an easy man to talk to and probably allowed us more freedom than any other Liverpool manager. If you had an important engagement somewhere which clashed with training, he was prepared to excuse you, providing that you gave him plenty of notice and did not make a habit of that sort of thing. He trusted us more than anyone else, allowing us to go our own ways as long as we did our best on match days.

One of the saddest sights I've ever seen came when our plane touched down at Speke after the Heysel disaster. Joe looked a broken man and Roy Evans had to help him across the tarmac into the terminal. Apart from the tragedy, I think it finally came home to Joe that he was not returning as Liverpool manager, even if it was by choice. I have never seen anyone so upset and I did wonder if we would ever see him again at the club. He has never told us what went through his mind, but it was a long time before we had any contact with him again. It was as though he wanted to purge himself of football and it was four or five months before we saw him around. When we did, he was more like the old Joe, the infectious grin was back and so was the bounce in his step. Whatever it was that depressed him fortunately departed and he was the old cheery figure that we had known for so long.

It's frightening to think that this game can have that effect on you but it has happened to other people in the past and no doubt will happen again. It was Shanks who coined the phrase 'Football is not a matter of life and death, it's more important than that'. Sometimes it's difficult to remember that it still is only a game because of the passions and emotions it can generate, but if we lose sight of that, we are in trouble, and I hope I can always keep it in perspective.

The first I knew about Kenny Dalglish taking over was on that silent flight back from Brussels. That is an experience I never want to repeat. When we had lost games in Europe in the past we had always been able to raise our spirits by looking ahead to the next game, but after Heysel the flight was more like a funeral. I suppose it was fitting that we felt like this; that short journey seemed an eternity.

We all wondered how Kenny would tackle the job, but it did not take us long to realise that he was going to bridge the gap between player and manager very quickly and effectively. Apart for the obvious change – that we were expected to call him boss – he also made his presence felt as a disciplinarian.

It can't have been easy for him, probably harder than it was for us, but he clearly decided he would do it his way right from the beginning. I had been recuperating all summer from my shoulder operation, and had been told that I would not be ready for pre-season training, so I arranged to do a couple of days coaching in Dublin, when the lads reported back. I rang Vanessa at home to see how things were, and she said that Kenny had been on the phone all day wondering where I was. She suggested I get back to him straight away, which I did, to face a carpeting from the new manager. Not the best way to get started. We had been next-door neighbours in Southport, and had taken it in turns to drive in for training, but now that relationship had changed, which was only right and proper. Kenny wanted to know why I was in Dublin instead of on the training ground with the rest of the lads. When I pointed out that I had not been given the all-clear to start work he said it made no difference. It was important that we were all together, fit or not, to prepare for the new season. I was left in no doubt that he considered that I was in the wrong and I did not forget it.

He was merely imposing his authority right from the start and who could blame him? He was taking over at a very difficult time for the club and who had ever heard of a player–manager for somewhere as big as Liverpool? He knew what he was doing, however. He left the training in the hands of Ronnie Moran and Roy Evans, and expected to be treated like a player at our training headquarters at Melwood. It was a difficult balancing act; to be one of the boys in the morning, taking his orders from Ronnie and Roy, yet the boss after lunch when they would do as he said.

It was not easy because he needed to keep some distance between himself and us, yet here was a fellow who had always enjoyed the company in the dressing room when he was just a player. It was something which had to be done, however, and we quickly realised he could be very single- 87 minded when it came to team selection. Phil Neal and Alan Kennedy both left that season, Phil to Bolton and Alan to Sunderland. That was a reminder to the rest of us that past achievements were not going to count for anything. This was going to be Dalglish's Liverpool and if heads were to roll, well, so be it.

He started off in the team but then left himself out, and I suspect that he would have been happier not playing providing that the team was successful without him. He has always kept himself physically fit and is an object lesson to any footballer when it comes to taking care of his body. We knew that every Thursday and Friday he would go to bed for an afternoon's sleep, so even when he was manager it was pointless trying to speak to him at those times, because unlike most of us he would have his head down. Still to be able to perform at the highest level at the age of 37, and as a striker more often than not, shows how he has benefited from the regular routine.

We knew it would be different with Kenny in charge because right from the start he told us he would not always play the same way. He was ready to change the team regardless of results, and to change the formation to suit particular games. During his first two years in charge he would never name the team on a Friday (another change in the Liverpool tradition), instead he always named a squad. This meant that on Friday night you did not know if you were playing, or a sub or merely a spectator. Obviously, everybody was kept on their toes wondering what he had up his sleeve.

I'm sure the fans did not believe us, but in his first year, we didn't know who was in the team until around 1.45 pm on Saturday lunch time.

In the pre-season games at Brighton, Bristol and Charlton, we used a sweeper system, which certainly helped me because strictly speaking I shouldn't have been playing at that stage. In this less physically demanding role I could cope – even with my shoulder injury.

Kenny was always prepared to experiment, rendering another of Shankly's famous sayings obsolete. The great man liked to quip to the press boys 'It's the same team as last season'. With Kenny in charge, it was no surprise if it was not the same team as last week even after a thumping victory. In his first season, there were so many changes, that apart from Ian Rush and Alan Hansen, nobody was sure of playing. Kenny did, of course, include himself in the long list of players left out at some stage.

He won the double in his first season and nobody was going to argue with that, but he did take some stick in his second season even though we finished runners-up in the championship and beaten finalists in the Littlewoods Cup against Arsenal. It's easy to attack him in print because Kenny does not go out of his way to make friends just for the sake of it. Really he is a very private person; his family comes first, and I believe he is at the most relaxed in their company. This might give people the wrong impression but I can't see him changing just to satisfy public opinion. When you do get to know him he can be very amusing, and generous to a fault, although he would not thank anyone for talking about the kindnesses he has shown to so many people.

He keeps himself to himself, and if people don't like it, well, that's too bad. That is the way he is and he believes in doing things his way. He doesn't talk freely to the press, but then he doesn't say much to the players either. His first priority is to keep the opposition guessing, and if that ploy is successful he will stick to it regardless of what others may say or think. It's been said before but it is still a fact – the dividing line between success and failure is very thin in this game. In Kenny's first season Everton lost the championship and we took full advantage in order to win it from them in 1986. The last time around the reverse was true, but Kenny did not look for excuses. He has never cited injuries as a reason, although last season was the worst I can remember at the club. Kevin MacDonald and Jim Beglin both suffered broken legs, Bruce Grobbelaar broke an elbow, Steve Nicol was out before Christmas with a hernia, and I ruptured an Achilles' tendon. All these were long-term injuries.

Kenny has not changed during his two seasons in control, unless he has become more protective towards the players. He has put on some weight, which we felt was fair game for a little fun. We started calling him an office worker, but he can take that sort of thing in his stride. Taking the mickey is one thing, questioning authority is something quite different. Kenny has always made a point of never criticising any of us in public, whatever he may have to say in the dressing room and we appreciate that. I can recall when we would drive in together as players for training, and he always said then that the worst thing a manager could ever do was slam his players in public. If we ever heard it happening on the radio Kenny would shake his head and say 'You should never do that no matter what the circumstances'.

I am sure he has discovered since he became a player–manager that he sees the game quite differently. It's one thing to be out there in the thick of the action and another to take a reasonably detached view – if that is possible – when you are watching your own team. I have never been able to understand why so many managers prefer to watch from the dug out instead of the grandstand. I have done both and would rather see the whole game instead of just the stocking tops. Clearly you need people close to the action, but I have been impressed by watching Jim McLean, the manager of Dundee United, on television, who makes sure he has a perfect vantage point but also a telephone to the dug out so he can pass on any instructions he feels may be necessary.

When Kenny first started as manager, and was playing regularly, I think he tried to do too much and quickly discovered it was not possible to do both at the same time. It didn't take him long to realise this. At half-time Ronnie Moran usually has the most to say, but Roy Evans and Bob Paisley also get their chance, and so does Kenny, and I think this affected his play in the early days. Either he realised it or somebody pointed it out to him, because he changed as the season progressed and by the time he was in the side on a regular basis again in the second half of the season he was one of our best performers as the magical double drew ever closer.

On the field he is quite prepared for anyone to have a go at him; if you felt something needed to be said he would take it just as the rest of us would from him or anyone else in the team. There was never any situation when you needed to think twice because you were shouting at the gaffer. What was said in the game was fair comment and certainly not held against you when the final whistle went. A lot of things are said in the heat of the moment, rightly or wrongly, and he understands that and encourages it if it is going to help the team. No one felt inhibited on that score.

Nobody needed to tell Kenny if he was struggling either, he was usually first to know. If the game was not working out at half-time he would make a few points and freely admit he was one of the biggest culprits, if that was the case. Don't forget, we are talking about one of the greatest players of the last 25 years; in fact, Bob Paisley goes further than that and says Kenny is the best he has seen in nearly 50 years at the club.

THE IRISH CONNECTION

I wish I had a pound for every time I have been asked whether I regret choosing Ireland instead of England for my international career. The answer is a very definite NO. I have enjoyed every minute of my involvement with the Republic; they are a great bunch of characters on and off the field who have provided me with more laughs than I could ever have imagined when I first joined them.

The Irish way of life rubs off on you whether you come from Preston or anywhere else; they live for the day which is a totally different approach from the one on this side of the water. Of course it's flattering to read in the newspapers that I could have been an England regular but when I agreed to play for the Republic I was not to know how my career would unfold, and there had been no hint that England saw me as a future international.

As a teenager playing for a Third Division side I'm sure I would have been a long way down the pecking order in England's plans whereas the Republic has always been on the look-out for players who qualified to play for them. There are all sorts of stories of FAI officials digging deep into the archives to prove a player's qualification and even checking out gravestones in isolated cemeteries in Ireland to prove a player's great-grandparents were buried in the Emerald Isle.

As an Englishman born and bred I take the inevitable wisecracks without any offence. 'His mother fed him Irish stew', or 'He once owned an Irish Setter', are the sort of jokes that are made about the many Englishmen who have opted to play for the Republic. At one stage there were a few murmurings in the Irish press that the English lads were treating it all as a bit of a joke, but that was never the case as far as I was concerned and you don't hear that kind of talk today. The Welsh manager, Mike England, didn't help either when just before a game between the two countries he said 'You only have to spend a fortnight's holiday in Dublin to be eligible for the team'.

Personally I don't think where you were born is important

anyway, so why do people poke fun at the Irish situation and ignore similar cases involving other countries? Nobody makes a fuss about Terry Butcher being born in Singapore and playing for England, or Liverpool's new signing, John Barnes, who was born in Jamaica and also plays for England. At the back end of last season Craig Johnston was put on standby for England, although he was born in South Africa and raised in Australia. Pat Van den Hauwe was born in Belgium, brought up in London, and plays for Wales.

On the continent it is even less important. Brazilians playing in Portugal have dual nationality and the brilliant young forward, Scifo, was born in Italy and plays for Belgium. Way back, the great Alfredo di Stefano played for Spain although he came from Argentina. Why then should the Irish be the butt of all the jokes? Perhaps it's for that very reason, that they are Irish.

It rankles that we had never qualified for a major competition before this season, but if you look at the other British teams, what have they won since England's World Cup victory in 1966? It is a sore point that we have not been more successful because, ever since I have been associated with them, the Republic have always had some of the best players around. Johnny Giles was the player–manager when I began my international career, and ever since some of the biggest names in the British game have played for the Republic. When you look at the present squad there is no reason why it should not make an impact. Liam Brady, Frank Stapleton, Paul McGrath, Kevin Sheedy, Ronnie Whelan – there is no shortage of top quality material available.

What we have consistently lacked is a goal-scorer, but not every country can boast an Ian Rush or a Gary Lineker. Frank Stapleton is a top class centre forward but not recognised as a prolific scorer, he makes as many as he nets, and our problem has been finding the right partner for him. Perhaps John Aldridge will be the answer now he is playing regularly for Liverpool. Certainly his record bears comparison with most in the First Division and I know he is desperate to make an impression at an international level even though he is another of the expats. The organisation has improved out of all recognition and under Jack Charlton we play more like a club side, which can only be of benefit. 93

In the early days it was chaotic, to put it mildly. On many occasions your itinerary would arrive through the post on the day you returned from a trip. It told you where to meet and where you were going; all that it lacked was the match result. It became a standing joke with the lads and so did the never-ending fixtures against Iceland and Poland. I have nothing against either country, but whenever there was a blank date we always seemed to play one or the other. I made my debut against Poland in Dublin. Again, only the Irish could arrange an international match for a Sunday. We had all played League football 24 hours earlier, before flying across, but thankfully those Sunday fixtures are becoming a thing of the past.

The problem, for whoever was the manager, was getting across to the FAI council that the game was the most import-ant thing, not the socialising. When Eoin Hand took over the arrangements did improve. Terry Conroy, his assistant, was based in England and between them they ensured that all the players started receiving the itinerary by recorded delivery. Why no one had thought of this before is a mystery.

It was on one of the Iceland trips that the President of the FAI, John Farrell, had all of us creased up with laughter. John is a lovely fellow and all the lads liked him because he was a straightforward guy and his title made no difference to him. He was the same John Farrell before he became President, and that rather grand sounding title did not affect him in the slightest. We attended a reception given by the Icelanders, and the host made a speech welcoming us and describing his country, and how they enjoyed full employ-ment and a high standard of living for such a small and isolated community. John was due to reply on our behalf and we could see he was a little nervous when he stood up. He thanked the Icelanders for their hospitality and then added that it was nice to see they had full employment because that was exactly what everyone in Ireland was striving for, full unemployment! Our hosts did not know whether it was a typical touch of Irish humour, a mistake, or a genuine statement of fact.

On another occasion John called the players together to discuss certain allegations which had been appearing in the Irish press and promised us all 'I'm going to find out who these alligators are'. Once, in Spain, we were playing a European championship game and we had to win to stay in the competition. We lost 2–0 and the players were all feeling dejected on the flight home when John stood up on the plane and made another one of his famous little speeches. 'Gentlemen, I am sure you will all agree we have had a very enjoyable trip, one of our most successful, apart from the result.' It could only happen with the Irish.

That game was a nightmare for Ashley Grimes. It happens to us all at sometime or another that no matter how hard you try it keeps going wrong, and Ashley was taken off in the second half. Instead of returning to the dug out he walked off to the dressing rooms. They were locked, so he spent the remainder of the match sitting in a corner of the stadium on his own. When the final whistle went and we all headed for the tunnel a very unhappy Eoin Hand spotted Ashley alone, and said, 'What's the matter with you? Do you think you are superior to the rest of us?' Ashley, deadpan, simply replied, 'Yes' and that broke the ice for everyone concerned.

It was on one of the never-ending trips to Poland that Kevin O'Callaghan earned top billing. This one was at the end of the season, a blank date for the Republic, so where else but Poland! We flew to Warsaw, but the game was being staged in a place called Bydgoszcz, one of the strongholds of the Solidarity movement, which was in full cry at the time. It was a five hour coach journey from Warsaw, and when we got there – well what can I say? It made Toxteth look like the Bahamas. The hotel was dirty, the bed sheets were never changed and the food was basic to put it mildly. You have to go to Poland to realise how tough life is over there. It's commonplace to see women waiting outside food shops, and meat is a rare luxury.

We were locked in a room in the hotel for our meals. They claimed it was steak at dinner, but it looked more like hamburgers and may well have been horse meat for all we knew. It soon became apparent that we had the place to ourselves, and we discovered that the FAI members on the trip were all staying in Warsaw – they obviously knew something we didn't. We complained about this and as a peace offering they said that on the return trip we would leave early for Warsaw, in good time to have a decent meal at one of the best hotels before flying home.

After an international match it is the custom to exchange gifts and the Poles presented us with small embroidered table-cloths which bore the date of the game and the venue. Departing for Warsaw the next morning some of the boys were complaining of stomach upsets, the result of the totally different diet we had been existing on in down-town Bydgoszcz.

The coach was very basic – no toilet – and we faced another five hour trip. Kevin, who was with Ipswich at the time, was caught short and not to put too fine a point on it needed emergency drill, and pretty drastic at that, to rescue him from a very embarrassing dilemma. There was nowhere for the coach to stop and nowhere for Kevin to go. He was stranded with his own very personal problem on a bouncing coach rattling over a pot-holed road, which did not help in his predicament. All the lads rallied round. Out came the table-cloths which were put to good use in rapid succession before being flung out of the window. Any Pole following that bus to Warsaw must have wondered what was going on. But nobody, least of all Kevin, was about to enlighten them.

It was in Poland that Terry Conroy got ripped-off by some guy trying to flog local currency. You could get up to four times the official rate, so I heard, changing sterling in the streets. Terry was rather pleased with a deal he had negotiated, but when the exchange had been made Terry was handed a thick wad of notes only to discover that apart from the top two the rest were all cardboard. Terry was quite a mover when he played for Stoke, but he never got near the tout who had conned him. The rest of us watched Terry dashing down the street on a hopeless chase, trying to find a guy who obviously knew his way around, while Terry was not too hot on a street plan of Warsaw.

If you want a change from Poland, why not Argentina, especially when the Falklands War is on! That was another of the Republic's little adventures. Another end-of-season jaunt taking in Brazil, Chile and Argentina, with a final game in Trinidad to wrap it up. Around South America in five minutes! Well, not quite but a sufficiently exhausting trip at the best of times, regardless of whether there is a war on.

ABOVE *Will somebody give me a hand? This ball is too big for me.*

RIGHT *My first appearance at Deepdale. I am the mascot for Penwortham Hill Rovers. Eight years old and already dreaming of the big time.*

LEFT *A member of Harry Catterick's Preston team of 1976.*

BELOW *There are a few familiar faces here. To Harry's left is David Sadler, at the end of the row Nobby Stiles. Have you spotted me yet? I'm second row, third from left and the chubby lad next to me is a youthful Michael Robinson.*

ABOVE *No wonder I don't look happy, the strapping on my right ankle conceals snapped ligaments. I was asked to play on to see if they would get better before being laid up for 14 weeks. The wonders of medical science – Brighton 1979.*

TOP *I don't care what your name is, the ball is mine. In action with Peter Beardsley before his record move from Newcastle to Anfield.*
BOTTOM *Getting the deep-freeze treatment. The towel contains a block of ice to ease a calf muscle injury after a game against Norwich in 1984.*

ABOVE *The real boss of the household – no not Vanessa, but Barnaby on his best behaviour.*

ABOVE *Rome 1984 and the European Cup final. Craig Johnston is favourite to get this ball but Kenny and I are there just in case.*
BELOW *The lull before the storm – Rome 1984 again and 120 minutes away from one of Liverpool's greatest nights with the penalty shoot-out against Roma.*

ABOVE *A world exclusive – Kenny caught with a glass in his hand! Alas, it's only orange juice as he toasts the 1984 European Cup win with Ronnie Whelan and me. But who is the other guy? Liverpool fans get everywhere.*

ABOVE *Bob Paisley holding the League championship trophy for the fifth and final time in his great career as Liverpool manager. A man of few words but possession of that trophy says it all.*

ABOVE *Mission impossible: Joe Fagan on his way to appeal for order at Heysel, Tony Chinn is on his left.*

ABOVE *Farewell to Ian Rush. Stamford Bridge 1986; another championship for Liverpool but the end of Ian's Anfield career.*

ABOVE *Wonderful Wembley. Victory over Everton in the 1986 Mersey Cup final.*
BELOW *No room on top. Coming home to celebrate winning the double and the party has already started.*

LEFT *No holds barred. Gary Lineker gets to grips with me in the Mersey Cup final with Trevor Steven an interested onlooker.*

ABOVE *Three Lilleshall survivors who lived to tell the tale. Steve Nicol and Kevin MacDonald when we were all fit and in the side which won the title at Stamford Bridge in 1986.*

ABOVE *Getting out of the way of Graeme Souness. It seemed safer to use John Deehan's back. Who needs a ball anyway? A League match against Norwich in 1984.*

ABOVE *Flying high for Ireland. An airborne clash with René Girard of France in a World Cup qualifier at Lansdowne Road.*

ABOVE *The Liverpool connection in Dublin. Ronnie Whelan, Mike Robinson and I before a World Cup qualifier against Russia which we won 1–0.*

The tour was arranged before hostilities broke out but as the situation in the South Atlantic became worse we all waited for the trip to be cancelled. But no, it was going ahead. In fairness, the English clubs and certainly Liverpool did not put a block on it, but it was obvious they did not want us to go, and we were not exactly thrilled at the prospect either.

As the departure date drew closer we realised that the FAI were going through with it. Eoin Hand was sent to Anfield to talk to Ronnie Whelan and me, urging us to travel. We both had a lot of respect for Eoin and perhaps against our better judgement agreed to go. However, a couple of days later we changed our minds and pulled out, as did a number of other lads with English clubs. Eventually common sense prevailed and the game with Argentina was called off.

The tour, what remained of it, was not easy for those who did go. The venue for the Brazil game was changed a couple of times, and when the game was played the Republic ended up losing 7–0. That type of result does not do your credibility any good whatsoever. You can't blame the lads who played, but if you are tackling a team like Brazil in their own backyard it's essential that you have a full-strength team on parade, otherwise there is no point playing the match. They travelled many thousands of miles on that trip at the end of a domestic season when they would have been better off taking a rest after nearly 10 months of regular football.

Today Jack Charlton is the manager, and we have come a long way in the last 10 years. Jack was not everyone's choice for the job. He had quit League management at Newcastle, and was well known for his hunting, shooting and fishing exploits as he appears regularly on television in that guise. A lot of people expressed doubts, not at the man's ability or experience, but about whether he was really interested enough to make a go of it. I think he has answered those critics now because our results with him in charge say it all. We could never get them away from home, but already we have drawn in Brussels against a very good Belgium side, and won in Scotland – that sort of thing never happened in the old days. I remember when we scored a late winner in Malta, the historians were digging out their record books to find out when we last won a game on foreign soil – it was as bad as that.

I missed Jack's first games in charge. He arranged an end-of-season tour to, yes, you've guessed it, Iceland. But the Liverpool lads had already booked a holiday in Spain to celebrate winning the double, so we were not available. The Republic did well, winning a tournament which also included Czechoslovakia as well as the host nation.

At the start of the new season Jack arranged a get together for the squad at Lilleshall. Ronnie Whelan, Jim Beglin and I were invited. Jack wanted it to be a two day session, but Kenny Dalglish insisted we be back at Anfield for Thursday morning to prepare for the next League game so Jack settled for a one day meeting starting at noon.

When we arrived there was no sign of Jack, but we had been warned that he was a notoriously bad timekeeper. We asked the receptionist what arrangements had been made for the Irish squad and she said none. Some of the other lads from Manchester United, Spurs and Oxford began arriving, but no Jack. We were beginning to wonder if the whole thing had been called off and someone had forgotten to notify us. We were all debating whether to leave and head for home, but no one was prepared to take the lead. Certainly not me because this was supposed to be my first meeting with the new manager.

Around 12.30 pm in walked Jack, followed by John Anderson, the Newcastle defender, who was beaming from ear-to-ear and obviously with a story to tell. Jack said, 'Hello', and moved on to the receptionist to be told the same story we had heard, a good half an hour earlier. No confirmation of any Irish football team due at Lilleshall. Eventually Jack managed to sort that out, looked at his watch and suggested we had lunch and started work around 2.15 pm. So half the day, our only day, was gone before we started.

When we eventually made it to the training pitch we could not find the dressing rooms, and when we eventually did, no one had a key. Jack called me over for a chat about my future with the squad. He asked me point blank if I wanted to continue playing for Ireland. I can respond to that kind of direct question and assured him I did, even though I had missed his opening games. Once that was cleared up he told me he intended to play in a certain way, which was different from anything I had been used to in the past. That was all right with me, he was the manager and I was prepared to go along with what he wanted. However, I did have a few misgivings, one being that at Middlesbrough and Sheffield Wednesday he was associated with the long ball game which was something totally alien to what I had become accustomed to with Liverpool.

When the session started Jack asked all the lads who had played in the Iceland tournament to go through the routines they had used in those games, particularly the set pieces, throw-ins, free kicks and corners. He left Ronnie, Jim and me out of this and then invited us to see what they were doing. He told the other boys to take us through the routines while he stood on the touchline. It had started to drizzle by now and Jack had a golf umbrella with him which he kept closed. I could not help but notice that while we were being introduced to Jack's ideas he had turned his back on us and was practising his golf swing with his umbrella! After about 20 minutes of working at the set pieces Jack turned around and said 'Okay that's fine, let's all go home'.

As we came off the pitch we asked John Anderson why he had been so amused when he arrived. Jack had picked him up at Newcastle and after asking how things were going at St James's Park he had switched on a tape in the car. Suddenly John became superfluous as the words on the tape started rolling. 'Splish, splash, splish, splash, this is the best way to catch salmon.' For the next 15 minutes Jack was totally immersed in the art of catching fish and John could have just been part of the car.

My first game for Ireland, I have to admit, did not feel like an international. Sure, the kit was green, Dublin was a new venue for me, and the rest of the players were virtual strangers, but first and foremost in my mind was the fact that I was lining up for just another game. That outlook soon changed when I began to feel part of the squad, and therefore part of the Republic of Ireland. In that first game when the Irish National Anthem was played I remained silent, partly because I did not know the words, but also because I had no wish to offend anyone. I remembered the famous occasion when Terry Mancini had made his debut for the Republic, and was lined up on the pitch with the rest of the team. After the first anthem Terry turned to one of his colleagues and muttered 'I didn't think much of that one'. The reply was instant 'Shut up you fool, that was ours'.

I've come a long way since then. I wear the green shirt with pride and I want us to succeed. I have come to realise how much football means to the folk across the water. No matter where we come from they treat us like kings. There is nothing quite like Irish hospitality and their support is quite exceptional. I have no doubt that now the Republic has qualified for a major competition our side will have the biggest and most enthusiastic following of any team from the British Isles. Maybe it's because they are deprived of top-class football throughout the season until an international comes round, but no matter where you look you will not find more loyal supporters. They love their football and we owe them something regardless of our birthplace. We wear their shirts and it has become increasingly obvious to me over the years how committed they are to us.

That's why I applied for the post of manager when Eoin Hand's contract was not renewed. Perhaps it was not taken seriously enough in some quarters because of my age, but I was very interested. I felt it would have been possible to combine the job with playing for Liverpool and I cleared it with Kenny Dalglish first before writing my application. I felt I had something to offer, I knew all the players, and I had my own ideas on how I might improve things. I had even got my assistant lined up, someone I knew and trusted and who thought along the same lines as I did. The more I thought about it the more I fancied a crack at it.

It's history now that it went to Jack Charlton, and three days after his appointment I received a letter from the FAI thanking me for my interest and promising to keep me informed of any developments. Perhaps that one should have come recorded delivery, too, and maybe it would have reached me before Jack's appointment was made public. I'm happy to play for him, however, and I intend to go into management if I can eventually, but in the meantime I hope there are still a few years left to play at international level.

I sometimes think the FAI bend over backwards to make

the supporters more important than the players. They know they can fill a plane wherever we go so from a financial point of view you could argue it makes sense. This makes some of our flight schedules very inconvenient, especially when you remember most of us are based in England. We have been obliged to go along with them to fit in with the requirements of fans and often what could be a quick trip gets stretched to four or five days which does not go down well with the clubs.

I can remember getting back to Gatwick from Malta late on a Thursday night with Ronnie Whelan, still with a long way to go back to Merseyside and all flights finished for the day. We telephoned Joe Fagan on that occasion and he told us to bed down at a Gatwick hotel and make our way back on the Friday rather than travel overnight by rail.

The annoying thing about playing for Ireland is that we have enjoyed some famous victories but have never been consistent enough until now. We lost 2–0 in Paris with one of our best performances, but even that trip was not without its amusing moments. The game was at the Parc des Princes, a superb all-seater stadium, if a little on the small side. Everything went like clockwork before the game, perhaps we should have anticipated there would be a catch.

The hotel was magnificent, the food, not surprisingly in Paris, was superb, and the whole squad felt very content as we prepared for the game. This feeling lasted until the FAI Secretary, Pedar O'Driscoll, arrived with our complimentary tickets. Every player receives a few before a game at club or international level to give to his family or friends, but for this match we were allocated just one ticket each. Why only one, we asked, at the very least two were considered the minimum. Mr O'Driscoll said the FAI did not anticipate we would want more than one because the game was being played abroad. I ask you, Paris! It's not exactly the other end of the world from London, Manchester, Liverpool or Dublin. The end result was that we had to contact a well-known ticket tout in England to buy extra tickets on the black market so our families could watch the game. Somehow I can't imagine Bryan Robson, Glenn Hoddle and company facing the same problem when England play in Paris. Put it down as another Irish experience.

One of the best for me was meeting a character named Mick Byrne. Physiotherapist, coach, man of many parts, you name it and he willingly does it for the Republic lads. He has become indispensable to a succession of Irish managers and has to be the most popular person in the dressing room.

On foreign trips he made it his business to be the manager's gofer, right down to reserving his seat on the plane. We played one of many practical jokes on Mick when we had been to, no guessing, yes, Iceland. There is a big US Air Force base at Keflavik where the civilian flights come in, so security is naturally very strict. On this trip Eoin Hand asked the captain if he could sit on the flight deck for take off, but had not told Mick. One of the other lads sat in Eoin's seat while Mick took the head count to make sure we were all on board. As the plane started taxying down the runway, he smartly nipped back to his own seat without Mick noticing. The plane gathered speed and someone called out 'Where is the boss, Mick?'.

A panic-stricken Mick checked the seat, now empty, where he thought Eoin was installed and shouted at a stewardess to stop the plane. 'There he is Mick, running on the tarmac', said another wag. It was only when Eoin appeared from the flight deck that poor Mick was prevented from having a heart attack.

On another trip behind the Iron Curtain – it could have been Poland but I'm not certain – we set up Mick with the stern immigration officers, who I'm sure are hand-picked to create the atmosphere of a communist country before you get out of the airport. Mick is a good Catholic boy but we pinched his passport on the flight over and substituted another, which had a range of pinups from *Playboy* plastered all over its pages. The fake passport was smuggled into Mick's inside pocket and he presented it at the passport gate with a big grin on his face. Our friendly officer immediately called a soldier over and after taking a very close interest in every page, very nearly carted-off Mick to the salt mines before we blew the whistle on the prank and returned the real one to him. Sorry Mick, no names, no pack drill on that one.

Something which never fails to amuse us when we are

playing in Dublin are the match tickets which give the fixtures, the date, the venue and, tucked away in the corner, the price of the ticket, say 12 Irish pounds, and in brackets 'including admission'. What else is on offer? We have never discovered to this day.

On a more serious note we all wonder why the Republic does not have a national football stadium. England has Wembley; Scotland, Hampden Park; Northern Ireland, Windsor Park and Wales has three good-sized venues at Wrexham, Cardiff and Swansea. The Republic, however, must rely on Lansdowne Road, the home of Irish Rugby Union. Don't get me wrong, as far as the facilities go, particularly the dressing rooms, it can leave old-style Wembley far behind; and when there are 50,000 packed in, which is usually the case, the atmosphere is fantastic. The pitch is a disaster for soccer, however.

It is not only the Rugby Union headquarters, but also the home of a Rugby club which plays on the pitch regularly, yet surely something could be done when there is a soccer international on the programme? Goodness knows there are not many in a season. The grass is always too long, the pitch is usually rock-hard and it just does not lend itself to a good game of football. The fact that there have been some excellent matches is a credit to the players of both sides. Any team which prides itself on being able to pass the ball will find Lansdowne a nightmare. We complain regularly and so do all the visiting teams. I don't think I have ever played there when there has been any give in the pitch, apart from the grass being too long. I don't understand why someone from FAI cannot spend a few pounds to ensure that the grass is cut and watered before a big international. It's not a case of helping the opposition, it could make a difference to the Republic team, too, because we like to think we can pass the ball well.

I can appreciate the FAI's problem. We have never qualified for a major competition until now and I'm sure they don't have the funds to build their own stadium but in the meantime they must get the agreement of the Rugby Union people to allow the pitch to be prepared for a soccer match. If they refuse the FAI must seek an alternative.

Before Lansdowne the regular ground was Dalymount 103

Park. The pitch is far superior, but the facilities are pretty basic by modern standards and the all-important subject of finance is also a factor. Dalymount is only half the size of Lansdowne, with only a fraction of the number of seats, so receipts are considerably lower. If we must stick to Lansdowne surely it's not asking too much for the Fire Brigade to water the pitch and for someone to be paid a few bob to cut the grass. I can't believe the Rugby authorities would object to that.

DEFENDERS – AND THE REST

I have always had a vested interest in central defenders, ever since Nobby Stiles pointed me in that direction as a player. It's probably the least glamorous position on the field because of the nature of the job. When people look at successful teams the players they probably think about last are the guys at the back. By and large we are regarded as destroyers rather than crowd pullers who produce the moments of magic. I'm not complaining about that and I can have few complaints about the way it has worked out for me. But I do think my fellow defenders who perhaps play for less successful clubs do not always get the credit they deserve.

When Colin Todd was in his prime, I was at a very impressionable age, and the memory of his ability has stayed with me. What struck me immediately about him was that he was one of the first who was prepared to carry the ball forward out of defence. Until he broke the mould, defenders were supposed to knock over the centre forward and bang the ball anywhere in the hope that more skilful members of the team would pick it up. The technique has changed since those days, and at Liverpool the emphasis is on playing yourself out of trouble and that is becoming the case elsewhere, too.

Todd was the first real footballing defender I can remember, and his partner at Derby, Roy McFarland, also put the accent on skill. I have never believed it was necessary for a centre half to be a bruiser, and the way the game has changed, it's vital for every member of the side to have pace and to be reasonably comfortable on the ball. That was Todd's greatest strength, even if his time at the top was not as long as it should have been. So this chapter is dedicated to the unsung heroes, the centre backs who could play well but never really got their just rewards.

There is no time to be flash when you are a defender and Todd must have been a manager's dream because he just got on with it and maintained the same standard game in, game out. Like some other defenders he also proved his versatility, because he could operate in mid-field and at full back, too. I know that playing centre forward or in goal is regarded as the most demanding job on the pitch, but they are not expected to switch roles, which is often the case for defenders.

I fancy Norman Hunter will always be remembered for the wrong reasons. Outside Leeds, the English public will point to his mistake against Poland at Wembley, which cost England a World Cup place. Again outside Leeds, his reputation was just as a hit man. Whoever coined the phrase 'Norman bites yer legs' did not do him any favours either, even if it was meant as a back-handed compliment. Sure he could clatter you and he played in a Leeds team which was one of the meanest around. Who would fancy facing Messrs Charlton, Bremner, Reaney, Hunter, Clarke and Giles on the same pitch? I doubt if there has ever been such a physical team, yet they could play well, too. No team could have been so successful by relying on brute force alone, and Norman, in my book, was a much maligned character. Possibly it was because he played in the same era as Bobby Moore who was a completely different type of player, but I think the comparisons were unfair. Bobby was rightly acclaimed as a great player, but I think the old North-South bias counted against Norman. I don't care what people say, it has always been there and still applies today and not just in soccer. In cricket I always think you have a better chance of making the Test team if you play for Middlesex, although I don't expect people in London to agree with me.

Today, the young defender everybody is talking about is Tony Adams of Arsenal. Sure, he is good and has plenty of time to get even better, but how many times do you hear the name Des Walker mentioned in the same breath? I rate the Nottingham Forest defender as a better prospect at this stage, but he never gets bracketed with Adams. If he played for a top London club I think it might be different.

Conversely, if Adams was with, say, Aston Villa or Leicester I don't think international recognition would have come so quickly for him. I would put Walker in the England team ahead of Adams at this stage, yet the Arsenal lad has already been voted Young Player of the Year and is tipped as a

future England captain. He may well fulfil all those expec-
tations, but if he was playing for a less fashionable club I
think he would have had a longer wait before he wore an
England shirt.

What strikes me about Walker is pace again. He is not
the biggest defender around but he doesn't struggle in the
air and he has the mobility to rectify any mistakes he may
make. Of the current crop I admire Paul McGrath, and
Richard Gough and Gary Mabbutt who worked well as a
partnership last season.

I'm biased towards the people I know best for obvious
reasons so Alan Hansen and Gary Gillespie would always
be top of my list. It's not my business to question why Alan
is not an automatic choice for Scotland, but it amazes me
that he has won so few caps over the years. I know his worth.
He has so much ability and is so comfortable on the ball
that he is sometimes accused of being lazy, but don't you
believe it. He has got it all, including pace, which is something you don't normally associate with him; put that down
as one of the penalties of playing at the back.

How often do you see a small mid-field player described
as busy? It's because they take shorter strides so appear to
do more running than a bigger fellow even when it is not
the case. I'm classed as being fast, but Alan is as swift as
anyone at Liverpool with the exception of Ian Rush. But
you get labels in this game. Think of matches you watch
and the number of occasions you remember a fair-haired
player or a left-footed one. They are the players who stand
out for most people whether they are the stars of the game
or not.

Gary Gillespie is another first-class defender and I'm surprised it took so long for him to win international recognition. Since he joined Liverpool he has made the squad,
but he has had to be patient.

One of the oddities of this game is that the so-called hard
men remain among the most placid of characters off the
pitch. Defenders who built reputations based on crunching
tackles had much more to their game than just muscle and
power. Tommy Smith was called the 'Anfield Iron' and really
could shake you up in a tackle, but he was also a very
accomplished footballer. The same applied to Dave MacKay

who will always be remembered for his barrel-chest and endless courage, but where does ability rate when people talk about MacKay? It should be near the top of the list. Which takes me back to Norman Hunter. Nobody had a sweeter left foot, but beyond Elland Road few will remember him for that. Perhaps it's because I look at these guys from a different angle; this is the position I play and I know what it involves.

I know from what Ian Rush has told me that he would prefer to face a so-called old-fashioned centre half who may try to intimidate him rather than one who can play well. You don't frighten centre forwards like Rush and Gary Lineker because they can handle that type of thing, but pit them against a defender who can think for himself and it makes life harder for the very best of strikers.

Paul Madeley was an example of that; he was a complete all-rounder who played just about anywhere for Leeds and always looked good, whatever his role. Madeley had the physique to dominate the penalty area, but he also had a keen footballing brain which enabled him to compete with the best around. The central defenders are a much maligned lot, and I can't see that changing. Whenever a British player is linked with a move abroad it's never a back four man and I doubt if it ever will be.

One player who caught my eye, but never played at international level, was Henry Newton. He was regarded as a mid-field anchor man but I saw him play effectively in the back four and I'm quite sure that he could have made the step up to play for England alongside a centre half. I always look for defenders who are comfortable on the ball and he came into that category. So did David Nish, who ended up at left back after starting out in mid-field.

These guys made it look easy when they played, just as Phil Thompson did at Liverpool. Phil was one of the slimmest centre backs there ever was, but that didn't stop him from going to the very top, skippering Liverpool and England along the way. Alan Hansen still talks about when Phil played in the Liverpool side which only conceded 16 League goals in one season. Phil was always one step ahead of the opposition; that was his secret.

His critics were not very happy when he got the job

of partnering Terry Butcher in the 1982 World Cup, yet England's defence looked very secure in that tournament and along with Peter Shilton, Tommo and Butcher formed the most effective part of the team. Even today, as reserve team coach at Anfield, it's easy to see why he did so well because he is still a good footballer. He was never found wanting at international level and despite his slight physical build he never had any problems dealing with big forwards. There were a lot of players who found the step up from club football to the international scene too much for them, but Tommo took it all in his stride and that's the mark of a good player.

We may never hit the headlines, but we are there to do a job and in my view we have progressed a long way during my time in the game. Playing centre back is a specialist role and because the game is so fast these days we have been forced to adapt to meet new demands. I think Liverpool can take a lot of credit for the emergence of the ball-playing central defenders and I'm sure the early lessons learnt in Europe were a key factor in that.

When I sat down to select my best team of all time I was surprised just how difficult it was to restrict the numbers to 11. It's a game everyone likes to play, but the more I thought about it, the harder it became. Maybe I am showing my age – I will be 31 in June – but my career spans some of the greatest names in the game over the last 20-odd years. I appeared in the same teams as Bobby Charlton and Nobby Stiles when I was starting out at Preston, and, thanks to Liverpool's European connections and my international career with the Republic of Ireland, I have bumped into some of the outstanding figures of the last decade, including South Americans, when Liverpool played in the World Club championship in Japan.

Immediately, many of my Liverpool colleagues spring to mind as viable candidates but I can avoid the trap of omitting any deserving cases by selecting my team on the condition that none of the current Liverpool men qualify. That way I can look Bruce Grobbelaar, Kenny Dalglish and Alan Hansen in the eye and say sorry, the rules for this line up exclude you.

The fact that the majority of my selection are foreigners 109 is not a criticism of the domestic game, simply that I have been fortunate enough to come into contact with the very cream of European footballers over the years. I think the record of English clubs in Europe, not least Liverpool's, proves the point that we can compete on equal terms with virtually any top foreign club side. But when you have the luxury of choosing from such a vast collection I'm afraid the home based men do take a back seat. I have not picked the 11 best players I can think of, I have deliberately selected the men who could operate in a well-balanced outfit and I like to think it's a team which could beat the world.

Let's start with the goalkeepers. If the rules were different I would have no problem nominating Gordon Banks as my number one because he will always be the king for me, but, sorry Gordon, I never played with or against you so you must be discarded. A number of foreign keepers were on my list even though the popular theory is that they do not compare with British keepers. I think this is a fallacy, because I have seen some magnificent keepers on the continent. It's a similar situation when people south of the border poke fun at Scottish keepers; once you get a reputation it's very difficult to change it, and the same applies when the Brits look at keepers abroad.

I would be more than happy to have the Russian, Dasayev, behind me or the ageless Dino Zoff when he was in his prime. Try telling the top sharp shooters in Europe that they were an easy touch. I am going for a home-produced keeper, however. Bruce would have come into the reckoning if he were eligible, but the three who stand out for me are Peter Shilton, Ray Clemence and Neville Southall.

Ray left Anfield as I arrived so you could argue that I have only seen him in action in the final years of his career and the same applies to Shilton. Of these two I would plump for Ray. He always struck me as a more natural goalkeeper while Peter is the perfect example of somebody who has worked tremendously hard to reach the standard he has achieved. Both are outstanding keepers, but for me both must make way for Everton's Southall. He is the real Mr Reliability. He doesn't have an obvious weakness to expose. Like Ray and Peter he is a good shot-stopper, which must be the first priority, but there is so much more to his game than that. He commands the penalty area, claims crosses and keeps up a non-stop conversation with his defenders.

It's all about confidence with goalkeepers; if the back four know exactly what the man behind them is capable of it rubs off on them. It's possibly the most demanding position because keepers are not allowed to make mistakes, if they do it's usually a goal, whereas the rest of us, more often than not, get a second chance to rectify an error. Neville looks the part; he is big and strong and you can see how much the other Everton lads rely on him. Believe me, it's a good feeling when you know the last line of defence is in safe hands and Southall epitomises that for me. Everton tend to play a bit square at the back, as we do, so the responsibility on the keeper is even greater.

Southall, as much as anyone, won the championship for Everton last season. He came back from a very serious injury and in next to no time he looked as secure as ever. Don't ask me why but Ian Rush always seemed to score against Southall while he never managed it against Manchester United. That is one mystery that will never be solved. I'm sure Rushie felt like the rest of us when he saw Southall prowling his line. How the devil do you get the better of this fellow? Rushie managed it regularly for Liverpool but I know how highly he rates the Everton keeper because they are team-mates together for Wales and Neville has played some fantastic games for his country.

Selecting a right back was an even bigger headache because there have been so many contenders over the years. I remember Danny McGrain when he was doing his stuff for Celtic and Scotland. He was much more than a full back, he seemed to cover the entire right flank as a mid-field man and a winger combined, apart from doing his first job in defence. He was strong in the tackle and quick off the mark. As I go through my team you will see that pace is always near the top of my list of essentials. It's something I have always based my game on and I think it is vital in every member of the team, including the goalkeeper, where quickness of mind is just as important as physical speed.

Another Scot, Sandy Jardine, pushed McGrain close for the same reasons. It must have been quite a sight when the old firms of Rangers and Celtic clashed to watch these two

111

in action, virtually doing the same job for their respective teams. For me they have been the top two in their positions in this country, but my other candidates come from the continent.

Eric Gerets, the Belgian now playing in Holland, is one, despite the bribes storm which threatened to end his career a few years back. I must be due a few bob, Eric, for putting you in the frame! The Frenchman, Amoros, is another and Camacho, from Spain, completes the trio.

I've gone for Gerets because he performs in the British style, more so than the other two continentals. He is physically strong, and takes no prisoners, and would have been quite comfortable if he had come over here to play. He skippered Belgium before his spot of trouble and was quickly installed as captain when he joined PSV Eindhoven, so clearly his leadership qualities have been proven.

Surprisingly, choosing a left back was relatively simple. I found I was short of genuine challengers for this role. Perhaps it's a fact of life that there have not been many natural left backs over the years, certainly that has been the case in this country. Kenny Sansom is an obvious exception; he has become a fixture in the England team and has proved his worth over a long period of time but I am being very selective and, to be honest, Kenny does not fit the bill for me. I admired Terry Cooper when he was at his peak and he would have been a serious candidate if he qualified, but I had no hesitation in naming Juventus full back Cabrini as my first choice. I cannot think of anyone else who remotely rivals him.

Cabrini hardly looks the part, I know. Small, with old fashioned long shorts, he is not the type to stand out, but after studying him at close quarters I recognise him as something special. When we played Juventus in the Super Cup in Turin, I appreciated his value on and off the field. Graeme Souness picked this fellow out soon after joining Sampdoria and I could see what Graeme meant when we played that match on a pitch that was far from ideal.

There had been heavy falls of snow when we went out to play that game, and there were serious doubts as to whether the match would go ahead. In fact, it probably would have been called off if we had not arrived on time. I've played against Cabrini on a few occasions and discovered how appearances can be deceptive. In his kit he looks more like Desperate Dan playing for some cow pie than a world-class full back. He wears his hair short, has an unshaven face and looks a rugged character, but there is quality there, too.

In that snowbound game in Turin he also showed a nice sense of humour. I came off at half-time with a thigh injury and watched the rest of the game from our dug out. Mr Cabrini came over to take a throw-in close to where I was sitting; he took his time because Juventus were winning 1–0. We all gave him a load of stick urging him to get on with the game. He just gave us a long hard stare and when the noise had died down followed it up with a cheeky wink. That's style. No reaction, no angry response and still time to find a little light relief in the heat of the game. It was a nice touch which deflated us.

Cabrini was telling us in his own way that he was completely in charge; time was something he seemed to have on his side. He was never caught under pressure and was always capable of playing the game at the pace which suited him. The biggest tribute I can pay him is that Juventus never appeared to play with a recognised mid-field player on the left-hand side, they left that duty to Cabrini, too.

Just as Cabrini was an obvious choice, so was one of my centre backs. As I have mentioned elsewhere in this book, Colin Todd has had a lasting effect on me over the years. When I was starting out he was always the one I most admired and no one I have seen since changes that feeling. He would be one of the first names on my team sheet, and when you consider how many others are worthy of consideration that's the biggest compliment I can pay Colin. The Poles, Gorgon and Zmeuda, are contenders, as are Terry Butcher and my Irish colleague Paul McGrath of Manchester United. The names of Rudi Krol from Holland, Bossis from France and Morton Olsen from Denmark can be added to that list. Franz Beckenbauer is disqualified only because I never had the pleasure of competing against him, otherwise he would be a top contender.

If I were to put Nobby Stiles in this company people might think that it was for sentimental reasons, but believe me, that is not the case. Nobby would rate a mention against 113 anybody, so would Roy McFarland, the Derby partner for Colin Todd, and Everton captain, Kevin Ratcliffe. I am looking for the right combination at the heart of my defence, and I don't believe you necessarily need a big stopper with a sweeper type alongside him. Todd and McFarland worked so well together that they were an ideal partnership and I've already admitted that I'm biased towards Todd. Some of his duels with Kevin Keegan were out of this world. Keegan and Todd would go at it from the first whistle – two men whose pace and physical strength were perfectly matched and whose personal battles would always be played out in the right spirit.

Whoever is to be his partner, Colin Todd is guaranteed a place in my team. I have gone for a number of attack-minded players and that's another reason to have Todd at the back. He had the pace to compensate for any lack of numbers if we happened to get stretched at any time, and after much deliberation, I have selected the Frenchman, Bossis, to partner him. I came across Bossis while playing for Ireland, and I think his qualities would dovetail perfectly with Todd's. I have always thought that Bossis was underrated, but because he is a central defender I have tended to watch his game more closely to see if there was anything I could learn from him.

In the last World Cup, France relied on a mid-field composed almost entirely of attacking players, which threw extra responsibility on the men behind them, but Bossis always seemed able to cope, even against the stiffest competition. He was the man who sorted it out when France had their backs to the wall.

I rate McGrath very highly, too. If he is not already one of the best he is destined to become one of the top performers. Of all my nominated men, Kevin Ratcliffe must surely be the fastest but he is a similar type of player to Todd and I have made my feelings known about him.

In mid-field I was looking for a four-man combination and here again I was spoilt for choice but I wanted a quartet which would be balanced and capable of operating as a unit. I could include Tigana, Platini, and Giresse of France and then need only one more to complete the line-up. But look at the competition for that fourth position; Zico and Dirceu from Brazil, Boniek from Poland, Cruyff, Scifo from Belgium, Gullit, who has moved from Holland to Italy, and, from the domestic game, Bobby Charlton, Bryan Robson and Graeme Souness.

If you are wondering what my connection is with the great Cruyff, I played against him in a pre-season match in Rotterdam when he had just returned from Barcelona. I mention that because Cruyff scored in the game and I also hit two into the net. That doesn't happen very often so I thought I would put it on record!

Back to the list of mid-field men; there's Johnny Giles, Falcao of Brazil, Liam Brady, Glenn Hoddle and, if I were pressed, I could think of a few more. Undoubtedly the most difficult task of all is whittling that lot down to just four. In my mind's eye I know what I would want from my mid-field, so the first name on the sheet would be Graeme Souness as anchor man. It's a role tailor-made for Bryan Robson, but if I were forced to choose between them Graeme would get my vote.

Everyone knows what a hardy customer Graeme is. They know he is an expert when it comes to passing the ball but he has never been given full credit for his defensive work. Graeme could protect any back four both by his presence and strength, and also by his ability to read situations. He is an absolute must in my team. I wanted two others to operate in wider positions and the fourth member to support the strikers in front of Graeme. Do bear in mind that my selected team would all have a specific role in the team and have been chosen for that reason.

I've narrowed down the list of players supporting the front two to Boniek, Zico and Platini. All three are capable of scoring goals and of coming through from deep positions, but I have chosen Platini for a variety of reasons. He seemed to have a built-in radar system – he knew what was going on even when he had his back to the play. Some instinct relayed to his brain exactly where to go and when, and he had a habit of arriving at precisely the right moment to do the maximum damage. He would pump 30 or 40 yard passes, which at first glance would seem to be going nowhere, until you realised, often too late, that he had anticipated that one of his colleagues would move in the right direction. As if by 115 magic, the ball would be perfectly weighted for them to cash in on a breakaway.

Platini seemed to know exactly where everybody was located on the pitch. Perhaps he did have eyes in the back of his head; at times that appeared to be the only explanation for some of the things he did. He would also give you the added bonus at free kicks, too. The number of times he had scored from dead ball situations outside the penalty box is a tribute to his accuracy and finishing power. I would encourage him to play as far forward as he wished because with Souness behind him I would be confident that the defensive chores in mid-field would be in safe hands.

To balance the team with someone to operate wide on the right was not a straightforward choice either. Tigana and Giresse could do it, but I went for young Scifo, who has played the role so often for Belgium. He came through at an early age, he is full of potential, and he has already displayed sufficient skills to be comfortable in this company. Bobby Charlton started out as a winger and could operate anywhere across the front line and I'm giving Scifo the benefit of the doubt and promoting him ahead of more famous names. To leave England's 'main man' out of this team was not done without some soul-searching, but I stress, I'm looking for the right balance and that's why there is no room for Bobby.

On the left side I need somebody who is comfortable out wide but who could also get forward in support. Giles, Charlton again and Brady could all adapt to this role, but I must have Cruyff in this team, and he did so much of his most effective work for Holland wide on the left. He is a world-beater in just about any attacking position and I'm sure he would fit smoothly into the role I have designated for him.

With Cabrini behind him, Cruyff wouldn't need to worry about working back to help out in defence and would be given a free reign to take on people in their half of the field. Having settled for Cruyff, I remembered the Russian, Oleg Blokhin, who was a specialist in this role, and Jan Cuelemanns of Belgium, another character who could perform right across the line – but I will stick with Cruyff.

The strikers are all that remain and Ian Rush got me out

of a hole by signing for Juventus thus making him eligible. Last season I would have opted for the Italian Altobelli because he is a regular scorer in a League where goals are hard to come by, but Rushie put a stop to that. Quite simply he is the best striker I have ever seen over the last 10 years and I am sure his fame and reputation will grow even more over the next 10. So despite many great names worthy of consideration I was really only looking for somebody to partner Ian. The first name that came to mind was Kenny Dalglish, because when he and Rushie performed in tandem on a regular basis for Liverpool they were an absolute nightmare for any defence. But Kenny is still registered as a Liverpool player so, sorry boss, that rules you out. But at least you did get a honourable mention.

Michael Laudrup, Paolo Rossi, Blokhin and Cuelemanns all crossed my mind as suitable partners for Rushie, but how do I choose between them? Lubanski and Lato of Poland were terrific performers, and Preben Elkjaer has always impressed me. He and Laudrup took the Republic of Ireland defenders apart in the World Cup qualifiers in 1986 and I include myself in that. Another Dane, Allan Simonsen, comes into the top bracket too.

In the end I ruled out Rossi because he is an out-and-out goal scorer, just like Ian Rush. I could not afford to have two men of the same style operating together and I've already stated that I rate Ian the best in that department anyway. Lubanski was coming towards the end of his career when I encountered him and finally I reduced the list to the three Danes. Elkjaer fascinates me. Jan Molby has told me quite a lot about him and he seems to be a real character. He is a heavy smoker, and that's a rarity in the game today, and he likes a drink and a good time, but he always delivers the goods on the pitch. Exceptionally strong on the ball, very brave inside the penalty box, I see him as the perfect foil for Rushie.

I know Laudrup is going to partner Ian in Italy but in my opinion he would get the best support from the other Dane. Elkjaer has a habit of getting to balls you don't expect him to reach. Many forwards make runs and get there too late either by accident or design, but when he goes for something he nearly always makes it, just like Rushie, and I think he 117 would be the perfect partner to take some of the weight off my number one striker.

Souness would be my captain and Bryan Robson would be the substitute simply because he is capable of playing just about anywhere and could be relied upon to fit in with this star-studded company. If Graeme had not been available for this team Robson would have gone straight in as the anchor man. It's a team with the accent on going forward but there is no way it would be intimidated, Graeme would see to that and Cabrini and Gerets can also take care of themselves. Nobody would get a tackle on Cruyff simply because, even today at 40-plus, I doubt if he would be caught, while my two men up front could also handle any physical test.

All I need now is a manager, and I have another little surprise up my sleeve. There are only three contenders and the least likely one gets my vote. Bob Paisley was my first thought but most of my team would have a language problem with Bob! Seriously, though, he does have the reputation to command the respect of my team and his deceptively relaxed style of management would have suited my star players. Nobody ever gave a better impression of being in control without making a fuss about it. I was tempted to go for Brian Clough because of his highly individual approach and it would have been fascinating to listen to his team talk if half the stories about him are true, but in the end I went for Guy Thys of Belgium.

'Who?' you may well ask. But look at Belgium's record over the years; they are a small soccer nation which always seems to do well. Qualifying for World Cups and European championships seems to be no problem for them and they usually do well in the final rounds, too. Mr Thys must have something to do with that. He is not a young man; he sits on the touchline chain-smoking and with an inscrutable, but always miserable, look on his face as though he has the world's problems on his shoulders.

Belgian football at club level falls short of that in Spain, Italy, West Germany and England. Belgium's most famous club, Anderlecht, usually fails when they meet one of the top club teams in Europe, and they have never been feared

or respected to the same extent as, say, Liverpool has. The

Belgian national side today, however, despite not being stacked with household names, has a track record which cannot be ignored. Ireland have met them too many times in recent years and finished up trailing in qualifying groups for me not to have a healthy respect for the way they are organised and prepared. I certainly give credit for that to the man in charge. He would not have survived so long unless he had some very special qualities.

So that is my team – beat it if you can.

Southall	– Wales
Gerets	– Belgium
Cabrini	– Italy
Todd	– England
Bossis	– France
Scifo	– Belgium
Souness	– Scotland
Platini	– France
Cruyff	– Holland
Rush	– Wales
Elkjaer	– Denmark
Sub: Robson	– England
Manager: Thys	– Belgium

THE REAL SOUNESS

Without doubt Graeme Souness is one of the players who has made the biggest impression on me throughout my career. The most common adjective used to describe him by those who do not know him well is arrogant and I admit I went along with that view when I was with Brighton and saw him only from a distance. You have to know Graeme to realise that the image is quite false. The right word for Graeme is style and there is nothing wrong with liking the good things in life. What made Graeme different was that he discovered them sooner than most of us. Inevitably he was nicknamed 'Champagne Charlie' because champagne is his favourite tipple and it did come as something of a culture shock in the early days to see the boys ordering a round of beer, while Graeme was enjoying a glass of bubbly.

It's no crime to aim for and to savour life's luxuries and Graeme has worked on the football pitch for everything he has got. He is a terrible loser – he takes it as a personal insult – and that explains why he is such a natural leader on the pitch, prepared to fight for his team-mates. He was always destined to become captain of Liverpool, just as he went on to lead his country. I think it's fair to say that Scotland have never been able to replace him in their team while we needed a joint operation involving Jan Molby and Steve McMahon at club level.

To outsiders he will always be remembered as one of the game's hard nuts but that was just part of his nature. To sell him short by ignoring his skills in favour of the muscle would be the height of ignorance. He performed at the top level and maintained his standards for so long because he is the most dedicated trainer I saw at Liverpool.

Nobody put more work into their preparations and I can only think that the years must be starting to catch up with him following his first season as player–manager of Rangers. It's not like Graeme to get sent off twice in one season, he was always too bright for that to happen, and he has been

sent off again this season. If his legs are beginning to feel their age, he will get caught in incidents which he would have avoided with ease a few years back.

Even in his prime at Liverpool, Graeme was not treated any differently from the rest of us. In my first season at Anfield he had had some trouble with his back, but declared himself fit for an important game against Tottenham. While he was missing we had put together a good run, but it still came as a shock to all of us when Bob Paisley named him as substitute, even though Graeme was sure he was ready to return.

By half time we were two goals down and during the break Bob turned to Craig Johnston and said quietly 'You can have a bath now, son'. On came Graeme to dominate the game completely and we salvaged a 2–2 draw. Graeme had proved his point when given the chance to play, but so had Bob, because if Graeme could be left out of the side there was no way that the rest of us could assume our places were safe.

Of course, he could be tough as many players can testify. In a League Cup tie at Highbury, Ray Kennedy was being given a lot of hassle from Peter Nicholas, who was catching him late with some flying tackles. Ray, a big fellow, but one of the most placid characters you could meet, eventually snapped and took a swing at Nicholas right under the referee's nose. The inevitable happened and Ray was sent off. The match ended in a draw with the replay at Anfield the following mid-week. Nothing was said about Ray's dismissal but he was eligible to play in the second game. With about 25 minutes gone, Nicholas, in possession, overran the ball just as Graeme connected with a tackle. It was the end of the game for Nicholas and he was carried off.

In fairness to Nicholas, he didn't complain, but later when they met in a Wales–Scotland World Cup qualifier at Hampden, there was another violent clash between the pair of them. Nicholas can take care of himself, too, and whatever the rights and wrongs of some tackles it has been my experience that the real hard men don't squeal when they are on the receiving end. An old pal of mine from Brighton, Ray McHale, can vouch for that.

Ray was playing for Barnsley when he sampled some of the Souness treatment. The Yorkshire club were enjoying a great Cup run before they met us. They came to Anfield in tremendous shape and earned a replay. In fact they could have won it in the last minute when Trevor Aylott missed a wonderful chance. They really fancied themselves for the return at Oakwell and we knew we were in for a testing night. Ray, now with Scarborough, performed a similar role for Barnsley, he was very experienced and a tough customer himself, but in the very first minute Graeme caught him with an almighty challenge and Ray was not the same for the remainder of the match. Later he described it as the hardest physical collision he had known in football; that was Graeme. We went on to win the match and he even scored a goal.

There is a theory that Graeme has a long memory and does not forget some of the characters he has met earlier in his career. That was the case in one match against Nottingham Forest when their Irish international, Martin O'Neill, limped out of the action at an early stage. There was no love lost between them from previous occasions and Martin was made to pay for that. Up at Roker Park in another game their defender, Shaun Elliott, shot beyond the track and into the advertising hoardings. There was uproar about that but Graeme claimed Elliott had been guilty of some misdemeanor against one of our lads so had to take the consequences.

However, as I said earlier, to classify Graeme as one of the villains and forget all his other qualities would be a grave injustice. Graeme admitted that when Steve McMahon was with Everton and Aston Villa he could see a lot of his own play in Steve's make-up. This did not save Steve from getting his marching orders at Anfield one day, but if it's any consolation to my current team-mate, he was a player Graeme could identify with and I know he will be pleased he is doing so well for Liverpool now.

Perhaps it was inevitable that Graeme would sample some continental football, although it did come as a big shock to us all when he announced that he was joining Sampdoria. He seemed a permanent part of the set-up at Anfield, but when you think about it, the life-style in Italy, not to mention the financial rewards, were tailor-made for Graeme.

Living in comfort with the sunshine on his back is just how

I can picture him, even though he did turn away from all that to return to Glasgow and manage Rangers. I am told that he has introduced his own ideas at Ibrox. Talking to Terry Butcher and Chris Woods when we met in Israel last summer, I was surprised to hear how strict a disciplinarian Graeme has become. He certainly did not learn that at Anfield, but you can't argue with his achievements in his first season in charge.

As befits a natural captain, Graeme took the 'off the field' activities just as seriously when he was at Liverpool. It was in Israel that Bob Paisley handed over the reins to Joe Fagan, and Graeme organised a whip-round amongst the lads to buy Bob a retirement present. He bought a beautiful clock and had it engraved with the simple words 'To Bob from all the lads'. There was nothing flashy about it because he knew Bob would not have appreciated a flamboyant gesture. He did the same with the Scottish team when Kenny gained his 100th cap. Graeme organised and bought the present with the minimum of fuss; something right up Kenny's street.

Basically Graeme is as genuine a person as you could hope to meet and will go to endless lengths to help you. He hates anything sneaky; if someone wants to say something to him they will earn his respect by saying it to his face. Returning from a game at Coventry one day someone threw a brick at the coach. It didn't smash the window but, as quick as a flash, Graeme was down the aisle telling the driver to stop while he went looking for the hooligans. That was his style. He hates cowardice of any form. The first time I met him he was sporting a black eye. He didn't say much about it but apparently he had been cornered in a toilet and it had taken four or five men to do the damage.

A more unlikely pair than Joe Fagan and Graeme you could not expect to meet yet they had enormous respect for each other. Joe rarely raised his voice in the dressing room and that appealed to Graeme. Joe was never impressed by anyone with a big mouth, and Graeme admired Joe because he could always find time for a laugh, which is not always the case at a football club. When he signed for Sampdoria he went to the famous bootroom at Anfield with two bottles of champagne to say his farewell in typical fashion. He knew   123 what to expect and he got it. 'Thanks for coming, now clear off because we have got a job to do here' was Joe's parting shot and Graeme wouldn't have expected anything more.

My profession at large has not had the privilege of getting to know him. That's why he has never won the Footballer of the Year award or the PFA's award because he has the wrong image, even within the game. Yet you could ask any manager in the land and I'll put money on it that they would give their right arm to have him in their team.

It was the same at the Kop at Liverpool; the fans rarely shouted his name. I think that may have been a back-handed compliment because they took it for granted that Graeme was going to play well every week. It was only when he misplaced a pass that you would hear some criticism. They didn't encourage Graeme in the way that makes other players feel 10 feet tall, but I'm sure the crowd already accepted that Graeme was a fine player and would stay in the spotlight whatever they did about it. Before I met Graeme I'm glad that I had come into contact with someone in the same mould, namely Brian Horton. No disrespect to Brian, but I would describe him as the working man's Souness. Again first impressions can be deceptive.

I came across Brian when I was still at Preston and he struck me as a real moaner when we met Brighton at Deepdale. It was only when I ended up at the Goldstone ground that I began to realise what an influential character he was. Brian had made it the hard way. He was released by Walsall and disappeared into non-League football before Gordon Lee rescued his career by taking him to Port Vale. He never looked back after that.

At Brighton we called Brian 'Bald Eagle' because he was going thin on top and had a penetrating gaze when he looked you in the eye. He became one of my best friends in football. Most of the Brighton lads had arrived from other parts of the country and he kept us together, while his wife Denise did the same with the other wives and girlfriends. Just like Graeme, he did not suffer fools gladly and he was obviously manager material long before he went to Hull in that capacity.

If Brian had a fault it was arguing too often with referees and he got his marching orders for that on at least one occasion. He was totally wrapped up in the game and our manager Alan Mullery could identify with him because he had the same positive approach. When Brian discovered that Brighton wanted to swop him for Tony Grealish at Luton it came as a real body blow because he loved it at Brighton. Typically, however, once he knew he was not wanted he was off to make a good impression on David Pleat at Kenilworth Road. Brian never won the honours to compete with Graeme, but when it came to giving everything for the team he could at least claim equal status with Champagne Charlie.

GETTING READY FOR ACTION

Footballers are often denigrated by other sportsmen for their level of fitness and I accept that we don't do as much work as, say, a long distance runner, a sprinter or a swimmer. Last summer Adrian Moorhouse made this point claiming that he trained twice as hard as any footballer for virtually no reward. He is probably right but if swimming is his chosen profession, and one which involves more concentrated physical punishment than football, then that is his choice. I can think of other sports which are not as demanding as soccer, golf for example, yet the financial rewards are greater. You don't need to be a fitness freak to be a top cricketer either. It is said that ballet dancers are the fittest of all and have the most punishing schedules, so if Adrian thinks he is getting a raw deal perhaps he should try talking to them.

Footballers are trained to play football, it's as simple as that. It is probably why, with the notable exception of Kevin Keegan, we have never shone in the television series which feature sportsmen from all walks of life in their 'super stars' competitions. By the very nature of our job, most of our strength is in our legs; as far as stamina goes, we can compete successfully with athletes on the track, but we are always going to be second best in terms of arm strength.

We also have to maintain a high level of fitness for longer than most sportsmen – along with Rugby League players. With the exception of around eight weeks each year we are training constantly because the football season seems to get longer each year. I am not looking for sympathy because we are well paid for what we do, particularly at Liverpool, but every season is a gruelling slog in terms of the number of matches you have to play, starting at the beginning of August and going through to mid-May.

At Liverpool, everything is geared to being fit to play for 90 minutes. How many times have you seen teams tire at Wembley in the final stages? The reason is that Wembley is the most strength-sapping pitch in the country; there is virtually no air on a hot day because the stadium is totally enclosed and it takes its toll on the players. Win or lose, Liverpool have never tired at Wembley because of the effort and thought that goes into our preparations. In the same way, the number of times we have won or saved a game in the final minutes has become something of a byword, yet the reason is simple enough, we can play for 90 minutes whereas other teams apparently cannot.

You don't need a 10 mile hike or concentrated weight training to get fit to play football. In fact, Liverpool's training, even in pre-season could never be described as strenuous. The experts reckon that we usually come into our own after Christmas, which is when many of the early pace setters start to fall away. Again what they do in pre-season and what we do may be a factor.

It goes without saying that skill comes into it. If a side is new to the First Division their manager may well try to substitute stamina for a lack of skill. But over a full season you cannot hope to get away with that. You can train a team of robots to run all day but if they can't use the ball they will be found lacking somewhere along the way. Pre-season training at Liverpool only feels hard because we have been taking it easy for a few weeks and a twice-a-day routine shakes up the system – which is what it is designed to do. I would hardly call it physically exhausting, however, and it lasts for only three weeks.

Liverpool's training programme is an education, which is why so many foreign coaches like to come and see us at work. There are so many valuable tips to be gained, some so obvious that they never occur to people until they see them put into operation. For example, whatever the weather we are never permitted to wear track suit bottoms, and the same applies to the coaching staff. The reason is that you don't wear them in a match, even when the weather is at its most severe, so there is no advantage to be gained from wearing them in training. See what I mean about simplicity? Nearly all the sessions last 90 minutes because that is the duration of a game. We always train outside regardless of the weather because the game is played in the open. Again, it seems so obvious, but many clubs do much of their work indoors.

The club lays down strict guidelines for training. We all report to Anfield first rather than direct to Melwood. A bus then takes us, in our working gear, to the training ground. After we have finished, everyone from the youngest newcomer to the most senior professional, has a cup of tea before getting back onto the bus to return for showers at Anfield. This is called the 'warming down' process. The coaches took the trouble to discover that there is less chance of anyone catching colds or chills by doing it this way rather than showering immediately at the training ground and splitting up for the day.

At no time are we without a ball in training and that includes all the pre-season work. Every Wednesday at Brighton we would work without a ball, often running miles as part of our conditioning – it was known as killer Wednesday – but at Liverpool you always work with a ball, because that is what the game is about. It's rare for any Liverpool players to be injured in training simply because tackling is banned and we don't play competitive practice matches. The object is to save your best for match day and not leave it on the training ground. It all sounds like stating the obvious yet I wonder how many other teams prepare this way.

The same applies in a game. We do not go hell for leather from the first minute, we always try to keep something in reserve so that if the opposition is showing signs of tiredness we know we have something left to give. Liverpool play a passing game and if you can do that properly it's much easier than chasing long balls all over the place and expending energy needlessly. Wembley is the perfect example of a ground which is suited to letting the ball do the work and teams who try to run with the ball there can expect to pay the price. When people in and out of the game ask what is the secret of Liverpool's long run of success, they would do a lot worse than consider these comparatively small points, because in the general make up of the club they are just as important as the major ones such as buying the best players available.

Match day at Anfield really swings into action 24 hours before the game. On the Friday we have only a light training session designed to loosen us up with nothing unduly energetic. On Friday night the boys with small children usually stay at a hotel to make sure they have a good night's sleep with no disturbances, but I prefer to be in my own bed and never have any problems dropping off. Bed time is around 10.30 pm and I am usually asleep by 11 pm.

On Saturday morning I have a little lie-in followed by a cup of tea or some Lucozade. I am a Lucozade freak getting through three or four bottles a week because I enjoy the drink and I genuinely believe it does you good. I rarely eat anything more than a piece of toast before setting out for Anfield where we are due to report by 11.30 am. A lot of the lads live in the Southport area, so we usually take it in turns to act as driver. Even at that hour there are always people outside the ground, particularly the Irish fans who have travelled overnight on the boat and have headed straight for the ground. I think they also know what time the players will be arriving and it is an opportunity to get some autographs.

Inside the club it is already a hive of activity. Karen is handling a non-stop flow of calls on the switchboard, catering staff are busy in various sponsors' suites arranging the lunches which have become a regular event before games. The players usually go into the Crown Paints lounge to chat to guests until it is time to board the coach and report to a hotel in the city where we always have our pre-match meal. The lads who have spent the night there are waiting for us and we have our own private room for our lunch. I don't eat much; usually I have chicken, but really I only pick at it. Craig Johnston brings his own meal with him; it is something he devised himself with chicken and special rice which he is never without. We don't spend that much time over our meal. The hotel staff know exactly what we want because it will have been ordered the previous day and everything is waiting for us. Some lads will have eggs on toast or an omelette, some will have nothing at all. Everyone seems to have their own little fancies on match day and you will see a wide choice of food on the table.

Baked beans developed into something of a cult when they arrived unordered at one hotel before an away match. It was Bruce Grobbelaar who volunteered to eat them and then proceeded to play a fantastic game so the boys insisted 129 he kept having them especially while his form was so good. Bruce, being the easy going type he is, was only too happy to comply. Obviously, potatoes in any form are out, as are vegetables. I have always believed that it helps to go into a game feeling hungry, it certainly suits me and I feel sharper and better prepared for the game on a reasonably empty stomach.

After the meal we go into a lounge to watch the football programmes on television. There are supporters inside the hotel by now but we always have our minder, Tony Chinn, with us so we can move about without any distractions. There is nothing more embarrassing than being with the rest of your team-mates when you have taped an interview for one of the soccer programmes, and you can expect to face a barrage of criticism and jokes, especially if you have made a mess of the interview. This is all designed to take our minds off the game, and it is a useful way of killing time before we return to Anfield. It only takes around 15 minutes to the ground and we aim to be there by 1.45 pm; by then the crowds are streaming in and the car park is filling up. This time we head for our own lounge to read the match programme or the newspapers. One or two of the lads will be checking the racing form and laying a few bets before Kenny starts his team talk.

As the game draws nearer so does my awareness of what is coming; I now adopt a philosophical attitude to matches – something I couldn't do in my younger days. The game is so unpredictable but now I can accept that. Providing I give 100 per cent and do as I am told, there is nothing I can do if fate lends a hand. Other players react differently, Ronnie Whelan had a spell when he was physically sick before every game, and sometimes during it, too. It's nerves and that's how the game can grab you.

By and large most of the Liverpool players are reasonably relaxed because we have been through it so many times before that we have settled into a regular routine, no matter how big the game. Nearly all of us are pretty quiet in the build-up, keeping our thoughts to ourselves and just waiting for the kick-off. There are no orders flying around at this stage – the coaching staff know exactly how we are feeling thanks to their years of experience at preparing teams.

In the dressing room the boss will announce his team and we will distribute our complimentary tickets for our friends and families, leaving them at the players' entrance or in the main reception area. Some of the boys like to get into their kit early but I don't. Ronnie Whelan likes to take a shower, so does John Aldridge, and Ian Rush had a spell when he soaked his boots in water before a game. Craig Johnston, Jim Beglin and Steve Nicol are usually ready first, and like to get out on the pitch for a knock about with a ball, but it is usually 2.30 pm before I start to change for a game. It is then that Alan Hansen will take the team sheet to the referee's room.

Bruce has his own routine before we go out. He likes to volley a ball at the light switches to turn them all out before we head for the tunnel and over the years he has become quite proficient at it. I like a rub down 15 minutes before the kick-off and so does Bruce. Roy Evans and Ronnie Moran will be busy by this stage with the massaging oil while other players will be strapping ankles if they have a slight problem, or doing stretching exercises.

Jan Molby is probably the most relaxed by this time. He likes to sit down with his legs resting against the wall but I don't think even Jan can manage 40 winks so near to kick-off. Sometimes the referee will come in just to check your studs and see if you are wearing any jewellery other than wedding rings. I have always thought this was a waste of time because, God forbid, if any player wanted to sharpen his studs he would still have time after the referee had left.

The last instructions from the coaching staff or the boss will be reminders of what to do at set pieces depending upon who is the opposition. When we move out Bruce always likes to be second in line behind Alan Hansen and Rushie prefers to be last. Nearly everyone touches the 'This is Anfield' sign which is just above the steps leading onto the pitch and the married players will kiss their rings for good luck.

I am told that one manager last season actually spat at the famous sign as his team filed out, but at least it proved that he had noticed it! It has been said that teams are inhibited by that sign as they go out at Anfield, maybe that has changed, but if it is worth spitting at it shows that some people are very aware of what it stands for. Maybe it was an act of bravado to show his team that they had nothing to fear. From our point of view it is a reminder, in case we needed one, of whom we are representing and how much it means to so many people.

I should mention one other little ritual that takes place in the dressing room if Kenny Dalglish is playing. He goes into the toilet and it is Steve Nicol's job to follow him and ask him the quiz questions from the programme – from outside the cubicle, of course. In fact the toilets are the busiest places before the game, you can put that down to nerves, too. At half-time there is tea for those who want it or Roy's own special concoction, and the coaches and the boss will have their say about the game. Ten minutes can sometimes fly by and I know that if things were going well the coaching staff would be happy to forego any break. On other occasions it can be a priceless breathing space to repair any damage that might have occurred in the first half.

At the end of the game very little is said if we have won. Some of the lads jump straight into the bath, others like me sit quietly drinking some tea and trying to unwind. If we lose various points will be raised but not in any great detail. The Liverpool management is not keen on after-match inquests, they prefer to give you the weekend to think about it, and open the real discussion at the start of the next week. It makes sense because your mind is still racing after a game and it is unlikely that you will take in everything that is being said so soon after the final whistle. Also things can be said in the heat of the moment which could be regretted later. I know that this is not the case at some clubs, but I believe that Liverpool's policy is right on this issue as it is in so many other ways.

The majority of players wander down to our lounge after the game, but there are a few exceptions. Jim Beglin and Mike Hooper, for example, like to get away as soon as possible once the game is over. There is still plenty of activity at the ground at this point; there are always people to show around who love to see the many trophies and gifts which the club has received over the years and which are displayed in one of the many lounges.

Sick children are regular visitors before the match, and

we try to spend as much time as we can with them. Many are terminally ill and if we ever need reminding of how fortunate we are just spending some time in their company gets the message across that there are more important things than football. Liverpool have always made a point of trying to help these children, many of whom have to travel a considerable distance to come to Anfield for what is often their one and only visit. Meeting them helps you put everything into perspective. We also tape between 20 and 30 messages a season to be sent to children who are perhaps in a coma or too ill to travel, and some of the lads regularly attend a local children's hospital just to show their faces in an attempt to brighten up the day for them. We do not make an issue of it, it has become a normal part of our careers.

Back at Anfield on match day the radio, television and press have access to the players' corridor and there will be interviews to be conducted after the game. Liverpool do not impose any restrictions on this, relying on the players' good sense to guide them, but I have often thought how easy it is to say something in the heat of the moment which you could regret the next day. That does not apply just to players either; I am sure some managers must read their comments the next day and ask themselves 'Why on earth did I say that?'. When the adrenalin is still pumping you are in a less than steady frame of mind and you can easily go on the record with something which you would never have said 24 hours later.

In the players' lounge some will have beer but I settle for a soft drink. We are careful whom we admit into our lounge after the game because the last thing we want is to have our ears bent by somebody who wants to go through the game kick by kick. We understand how they feel, especially if it has been an incident-packed game, but players just want to slow down, catch their breath and put the match behind them. We have a rota system whereby three players go to the Crown Paints lounge after each game to mix with the sponsors' guests and have their pictures taken. It is all part of the exercise to promote closer contact with the public, and if there is a particular sponsor for a particular match they will ask for a player to attend their private lounge upstairs.

Most of us are ready to leave an hour after the game but this is often the toughest bit. There will be hundreds of fans waiting outside for autographs and getting away is often easier said than done. I have a regular routine in which I will not sign autographs until I have got into my car. It makes sense really, because if you are surrounded inside the car park it doesn't take long to get your clothes covered in biro as you are jostled by eager youngsters. You can get trampled on and your shoes can finish up in a worse state than your football boots. At least in the car you can take the books one at a time through the window and that way you have a little comfort and space.

Saturday night is time for a meal, particularly as I have barely eaten all day. Again because so many of us live close together it is a regular event for half a dozen of us to meet with our wives and girlfriends. Obviously the mood will be dictated by the result of the game. None of us are good losers and Vanessa understands me well enough to let me work it out of my system before getting into a proper conversation. My favourite Saturday night drink is a good pint of Guinness and I usually settle for steak for my meal. Saturday nights wind up soon after midnight when I am ready for bed and the one real lie in of the week.

I will make the tea on Sunday morning and take the newspapers back to bed providing there is no injury problem that needs attention. It's by Sunday that the aches and pains become evident and Ronnie and Roy will be at the ground by 10.30 am. They work a seven day week and if you have an injury or a doubt about fitness you must report in on Sunday morning. We have enough sense to realise that it would be foolish to pretend we are fine if we aren't because it is for our own benefit as much as the club's to keep fit. If I am uninjured I might pop down to the pub for a pint at lunch time or in the evening. Otherwise it is a real rest day for me when I try to do as little as possible.

You never know on the day of a game what is going to happen. When I ruptured my Achilles' tendon I spent the night in hospital; I was luckier than Kevin MacDonald who was stuck down in Southampton for a few days after breaking his leg. I had agreed to attend a summer coaching programme in Nairobi on the very day I sustained my injury against Wimbledon. Perhaps it was tempting fate to look so far ahead but if you go into a game thinking about injuries your whole life can come to a stop. We all accept that they are part and parcel of the game and there is nothing you can do about them. My most serious injuries have always been complete accidents; there was nobody near me when I caught my heel in the turf in the game against Wimbledon. I dislocated my shoulder for the first time playing for Ireland when I fell awkwardly and my stress fracture against Oxford was caused by a harmless tackle which just caught my leg at the wrong angle.

Nobody wants to leave Liverpool because anywhere you go after Anfield must be a backward step and while you are there you are looked after better than you would be anywhere else. If you are in the side the financial rewards are second to none but players do sometimes leave by choice and, I suspect, regret it later.

I still find it hard to believe that Alan Kennedy finished up at Hartlepool just three years after playing in a European Cup final. I believe he left prematurely and mainly because he was not in the team at the time. Players are not as greedy as they are sometimes portrayed. Everyone wants to be in the team but because there are so many top class performers at a club like Liverpool it is inevitable that some players will be disappointed. The easy way out is to sit tight, secure in the knowledge that you have a contract which is the envy of 90 per cent of your fellow professionals in the country but the need to play sometimes outweighs the security and rewards. I am sure that is why Alan left for Sunderland where he had an unhappy time before joining Hartlepool on a free transfer in the summer.

David Hodgson is another player who must be wondering if he did the right thing. He came from Middlesbrough as one of the most sought-after strikers in the country but he went back to the North East for a frustrating spell with Sunderland before joining Norwich on a free transfer. Hodgson left Carrow Road 12 months later and I am sure it has crossed his mind that he should have stayed at Liverpool.

JOIN LIVERPOOL AND SEE THE WORLD

One of the big bonuses of playing for a club like Liverpool is that you get to see parts of the world which would normally only be names on a map if you were engaged in any other business. Unfortunately European football is now closed to us but we still get away to play friendly games and pre-season warm ups. Before the Heysel tragedy, Liverpool had appeared in every European country except Albania in 21 years of uninterrupted competition and we have travelled to even further-flung destinations during my time at Anfield.

One memorable trip was to Swaziland at the end of Joe Fagan's first season in charge, during which we had won three trophies, including the European Cup in Rome. You get accustomed to hectic timetables but this was something else. The celebrations in Rome went on far into the night after Alan Kennedy's penalty kick won the match. The flight back to Liverpool the next day was merely a continuation of what had gone on the night before so by the time we arrived back on Merseyside we were really fit for nothing. We were setting off the next day for Africa with a 12 hour flight on the agenda, and if the truth were known none of us really wanted to go to Swaziland where we were due to play two matches against Spurs, especially at the end of what had been a fantastic season even by Liverpool standards. It turned out to be a trip not to be missed, however.

We staggered onto the plane on Friday morning nursing king-size hangovers and feeling physically and mentally exhausted by the game in Rome and the aftermath. Before the flight from Liverpool to London took off there was a delay and before we knew it a steward appeared with more beers for the boys. It was the last thing we needed, but just to kill time we all decided to have a couple which was like topping up from Wednesday night and Thursday. We were on a high without alcohol so by the time we reached Heathrow we were really flying again without the aid of a plane. We were travelling via Johannesburg on the next stage of the journey and again we had some time to kill before our flight was called, so it was back to the bar for a few more. We continued, hangovers long forgotten, with a steady intake on the long flight to South Africa, changing at Johannesburg for the connection to Swaziland.

When we eventually arrived there was the usual reception and more drinks. Put our week together, not least the alcohol consumed, and we were probably in the worst possible state of mind and body to play even a friendly match. We checked in on Saturday lunch time with the first game due to be played the next day. Spurs had come out earlier in the week and even managed a few training sessions in preparation for the games. Our lads divided into two groups; some just wanted to crash out and sleep off the effects of three of the most exciting days of their lives while others opted for some sunbathing. A hotel chain had arranged the games and guests were pouring in on the Saturday night, and we were all expected to show our faces as part of the promotion. At no stage did we do any training, partly because there was no time, but more significantly because we were not in a condition to do any!

On the Sunday morning Joe Fagan allowed us a lie in until 11.30 am in a belated attempt to have us rested and capable of giving Spurs a game. Taking everything into consideration, there was no way we should have been able to give Spurs anything like a decent game, yet we won 5–2! Even one of the Spurs goals was a Bruce classic. As he threw the ball out to one of our players it went straight to Danny Thomas who trapped it, and then chipped it over Bruce's head into the net. Bruce was our most famous player in Africa, coming from nearby Zimbabwe, and he was the focus of attention so we could not help ourselves when he dropped his bloomer. It must have been difficult for the spectators to understand why Bruce's team-mates roared with laughter at his mistake. But we were well in front at that stage and it didn't affect the outcome of the game. One way and another Joe Fagan was pleased that we had managed to put on a decent show despite everything that had preceded it, and we were given free time for the remainder of the week before we were due to play Spurs again.

Steve Nicol came out after the rest of us and typically got himself into a jam. When he arrived at Johannesburg he 137 tore up his flight ticket and threw it into the waste paper basket not realising there was another leg of the trip still to come to reach Swaziland. So when his flight was called there was Steve all alone in strange surroundings and minus a ticket. There was a panic-stricken phone call from the airport to our hotel before Steve was able to board the plane to join the rest of the boys.

On the Sunday night there was a cabaret at the hotel with the top American singer O. C. Smith. He had had a big hit with 'Hickery Hollow's Tramp' and when we filed in, in very high spirits, we adopted O.C. for the night. We gave him a standing ovation as soon as he came on and he could hardly believe it. After every number it was the Liverpool team which led the applause and by the end of the evening he was dedicating songs to us. Maybe his agent should get him a booking at Liverpool or Southport because he would be assured of a great welcome from the boys.

The following weekend was slightly different. An Australian named Roland Storm, a singer-cum-comedian, was top of the bill and I regret to say we absolutely murdered him. Give Merseyside a miss, Roland. Unfortunately for him most of us had heard his gags before and just as he was reaching the punch line somebody would shout it out. What he must have thought was nobody's business. It is one thing to take the mickey out of people you know but poor Roland must have wished he had stayed in Australia. We all received a polite but firm reprimand from the hotel management after our performance. After all, they had paid for the poor guy to perform and we had probably wrecked his reputation as far as Africa was concerned.

We knew we had the whole week to ourselves and it was a question of what to do with it. The hotel had everything – a swimming pool, casino, golf course, tennis, bowls, squash – you name it, it was all there. As if that were not enough, we had the option of going down to Durban for a few days in a couple of chartered planes. Bruce, one of our world-wide travellers, knows the city well and said that it was a trip we should not miss. So 10 of us piled into two small aircraft for the one and a half hour flight; it was one of the most breathtaking experiences I can remember. We flew low over the Indian Ocean following the coast down to Durban and the sheer beauty of the scenery takes some beating. Normally, footballers on aircraft spend their time playing cards, sleeping or having the inevitable beer, but this was something completely new, flying down to Durban in a tiny propeller driven plane and just drinking in the spell-binding views.

We were staying in another magnificent hotel in Durban and were asked to attend a cocktail party to meet some of the local dignitaries on our arrival. In return for that we were given free accommodation in this beautiful city. When the bar closed on our first night we were ready to see the sights and were recommended to another hotel nearby which had a night club. There was an outside lift to the disco which was situated on the thirty-ninth floor. As the lift ascended we were treated to another mind-boggling view across the ocean and the city, as we stood looking out through a pane of glass which was all that separated us from a big, big drop. David Hodgson started jumping up and down just for a joke but the lift was so sensitive it promptly stopped somewhere between the seventeenth and eighteenth floors. Suddenly we all took four paces back to get away from the glass because the view did not seem so appealing when we were stuck half way up a skyscraper. It did not move for 30 seconds but everyone inside would swear it seemed more like 30 minutes before it automatically re-started and continued its climb. I am sure outside lifts are as safe as any others but after that experience I have made a point of avoiding them.

Our five days in Durban will not be forgotten easily. It is one of the most spectacular places I have seen and I wouldn't have missed it for anything. We played golf one day on a course right alongside the ocean with monkeys darting in and out of the trees on the other side. It all smacked of paradise until we saw the other side of South Africa.

On the beach one section was fenced off for blacks, another for coloureds because there is a large community of Indians living in the Durban area, and another for whites. That was our first introduction to South Africa's biggest problem and I admit that it came as a shock. In Swaziland we had seen no evidence of friction between blacks and whites but here was a reminder of what really went on. Near

139

the hotel was an off-licence with two separate entrances marked whites and non-whites. What a tragedy that such a magnificent country should be blighted in this way. We were treated like kings throughout our stay but it does pull you up short to discover that not all the people of that country enjoy the same privileges and freedom. I am not a political person but what I saw made me think very carefully and I have not forgotten it.

One night we were invited to a restaurant by the beach called the Cattleman's Eating House. The owner wanted some publicity in the local newspaper so we all agreed to attend and had an excellent meal. When we had finished and posed for some pictures for the local press we were recommended another place to continue the night out. The owner offered to lend Bruce his car. It turned out to be a sawn-off two-seater open-top Mini. Bruce loved it but there was no room for anyone else to get in so we hired taxis and Bruce was to follow us. Now, he knows his way around Durban so he overtook us in his toy car and just as he was waving us good-bye we turned sharp left and Bruce sped on into the distance wondering where we had gone. Being Bruce, he did catch up with us later – it was a good job it was not Steve Nicol in the Mini because he might still be stuck in Durban trying to find us.

Durban has everything for a super holiday, including surfing. Craig Johnston was always telling us what an expert he was from his time in Australia when he would go out even with a threat of sharks in the area. One of the most humiliating episodes he suffered was trying unsuccessfully to demonstrate his prowess in Durban where he continually fell off the board. He eventually gave it up as a bad job and blamed it on the big waves. Never mind, Craig we believe you when you say you did it in Aussie!

Coming back from Durban to Swaziland we flew low over the soccer ground and there were the poor Spurs players on yet another training session. They could see us waving to them and must have wondered why they had to sweat it out under the African sun while we were joy-riding all over the place. It was rough on them, particularly after the result of the first match, but at least they gained an honourable draw when we met a second time.

In between the games there was a big dinner organised by the local Rotary Club where Spurs showed us up. They had brought various souvenirs with them, such as autographed shirts, and footballs to distribute but we had not been told to bring anything. It took us all our time to rustle up a solitary football and hastily autograph it. We were not exactly prepared for a semi-formal occasion either. The Spurs lads all looked extremely smart in their suits and ties while we had come strictly for a sunshine holiday with the minimum of gear. The Rotary Club was staging a raffle for the souvenirs so Alan Hansen, Steve Nicol and Gary Gillespie went along as our representatives looking as presentable as possible in the circumstances. The rest of us were still in Durban.

Apparently when the Liverpool ball was raffled a lady at the very far end of the room had the winning ticket and signalled she was on her way down to collect it. But Alan, who had drawn the lucky ticket, saved her the trouble by half volleying the ball across all the tables in her direction. It must have been one of his better efforts because no glasses were broken as the ball skimmed through the room, and to prove it was no fluke he asked for the ball back and did exactly the same thing again.

The week in Swaziland was one of the highlights of my career with Liverpool and so was a trip to Bangkok and Hong Kong but for different reasons. That one happened at the end of Bob Paisley's last season in charge, a year before our African adventure. You will not find the name of Robbie Savage in the history books as a goal-scorer for Liverpool, yet on that trip he hit one of the most stunning goals I have ever seen. We were playing Bulova in Hong Kong and they had Pat Jennings guesting for them. I bet even the great Pat remembers Robbie's effort, it was such an outstanding goal. Robbie never made the first team at Liverpool before moving on to Stoke, Bournemouth, Bradford City and Bolton but he was a useful mid-field player with an excellent left foot. The rocket which flashed past Pat came from his right foot and reminded me of one of Alan Mullery's spectacular volleys which was shown on television on many occasions.

You can buy some fabulous silk in Hong Kong and most of the boys went to a tailor's shop to get fitted for shirts and suits. Alan Hansen is an awkward shape, a bit like me, all legs and arms, but he got measured for a very snappy jacket by the tailor, Victor Chan. When Alan saw the end result he did not like it and decided to leave it behind but Mr Chan had other ideas and turned up at our hotel on the day we were leaving for Thailand. 'Where is Mr Hansen?' he asked. Nobody knew until we discovered him hiding on the coach hoping to get away unnoticed.

The flight to Thailand was the worst of my life. We got caught in the middle of a violent thunderstorm and the lightning was bouncing off the wings of the plane. I really did think we would never land safely. I admit that I started to say my prayers, and Tom Saunders, one of the backroom staff at Anfield and one of its most respected figures, gripped me so tightly that the knuckles on his hand turned white. Why is it, I wonder, that I always feel safer in a British plane? Watching the activity on that flight did nothing to reassure anyone. We knew it was getting tricky when the stewardesses abandoned what they were doing to strap themselves in, too. I remember the runway at Bangkok was flooded when we thankfully did touch down, and I sat in the VIP lounge counting my blessings. It was a really frightening experience and for someone who does not normally worry about flying a salutary lesson not to take anything for granted.

A lot of footballers have an aversion to flying. Alan Kennedy and my Irish team-mate David Langan suffer worse than anyone I have known. Alan was half cured on one of our European trips. Liverpool like to fly Aer Lingus when they charter and the cabin crew and flight officers have become our friends over the years. One of the pilots, Barney Cronan who was well known to the team, installed Alan on the flight deck for one take off and took him through every detail. When Alan could see exactly what was going on, and that the captain knew what he was doing, it went a long way to soothing his nerves but I can understand the agonies some of the guys go through. David Langan breaks into a cold sweat even before take off. His arms go rigid and he refuses to let go of the arm rests when the plane starts to move. Somehow I don't think he will ever come to terms with flying.

Is there any other football club except Liverpool that can claim to have its own travelling gynaecologist? Talk about covering every eventuality. Dr Winifred Francis has been a Liverpool supporter for many years and was a regular on our trips into Europe and it was through her that we found ourselves playing in Khartoum a few years ago. Apparently one of her patients was the wife of President Numeiri, and quite by chance the subject turned to soccer on one of her visits. The President's wife revealed that her husband was a big fan, one thing led to another, and before we knew it we were off to Sudan for a surprise trip just before Christmas.

There were all sorts of stories going round that the President was sending his personal jet to take us to Khartoum one cold Sunday morning. The day before we had played at Aston Villa and won well on a difficult pitch, but when we arrived at Speke Airport the only plane visible was a British holiday jet. We discovered that the President had hired it for the trip with no expense spared. In a matter of hours we were transported from a freezing December day in England to the glaring sunshine of Sudan. But if the weather was good, the country proved to be an enormous shock.

Without doubt it must be the most deprived country I have ever seen. To see women washing clothes in the filthy River Nile and families living in the very depths of poverty brought it home to us how fortunate we all are. We went on a short excursion to a local market and to see the poor quality of the goods on display was another example of how difficult it was just to exist in this sad place. When news of the dreadful famine in Ethiopia filtered through we could understand the implications because Sudan, their next door neighbour, was faring little better from what we saw. Around 40,000 people still managed to find the money to come to the game, however, and we were given a very testing work out by the local team and needed a late equaliser from Kenny Dalglish to save our faces.

It was very much a whistle-stop trip. Out on Sunday, play Monday and home for tea on Tuesday. On the Monday night after the game we were guests of the British Embassy club and I have often wondered if their precious snooker table survived our visit. Somehow some talcum powder found its way onto the baize and from my limited experience of the 143 tables I know how difficult it would be to remove it. We had a television crew with us on that trip and on the journey home we stopped in Athens to refuel and record a Christmas message for the folks back home.

Despite the memory of what we had seen there was still time for a few laughs on the return flight. Sammy Lee was bundled into a luggage rack above the seats and the lid closed and that was recorded for posterity by the cameras. I have often thought about the morality of being given the VIP treatment all the way to Khartoum and back when its inhabitants have so little. It does seem wrong that one of the poorest nations on earth should spend so much money staging a football match. Despite the huge cost of chartering a jet for three days we heard that the game actually made a profit after all the expenses and I just hope it went to the right people. We all met the President but a year or so later he was deposed so I doubt if we shall be invited back in the future.

Another long distance excursion took us to Dubai to play Glasgow Celtic. I had sold my house in Southport to a businessman who was working in Dubai at the time, so when we got out there he and his wife were able to show me the sights; you cannot beat having your own personal guide when you visit a strange place. We won the game on penalties and also enjoyed some lavish hospitality. There were problems on the trip home, however. Both teams travelled together but within minutes of taking off from Dubai the captain reported a technical problem and we put down in Bahrain. There it was discovered that the plane had a fault in one of its engines, and the delay would be between six and eight hours. There was only one way to kill the time and we filed into the bar for what promised to be a long session.

To keep ourselves amused we invented a Tube of the Year award to go to the player who had made the most memorable remark that season for all the wrong reasons. After a recount the winner was judged to be Kevin MacDonald, although I can't remember what it was he was supposed to have said that was so memorable. It was all a bit of harmless fun, no doubt inspired by the considerable liquid intake, and when Kevin stood up to receive his award Paul Walsh picked up one of the massive ash trays in the bar for a mock presentation. But one of the security guards took exception to this and threw us all out!

We knew it could be rather volatile in that part of the world but this seemed a little excessive especially when he called us a bunch of hooligans. Eventually we drifted back into the bar in twos and threes and there was the same guard with his gun in his holster. But it was a long wait and by the time it was over he had relented and was even helping the guy behind the bar to serve the drinks. That weekend we had a convincing win over Chelsea while Celtic struggled to get a draw and their manager David Hay was quoted as saying 'We shall have to drink as much as some of the Liverpool players next time because that seems to be the secret of their success'.

It would be wrong of me to convey the impression that playing for Liverpool is one long round of drinks. That is not the case, but we do know how to enjoy ourselves when the occasion arises and I must say that the club doesn't place any restrictions on us when we are involved in friendly matches. We know when to draw the line, however. Playing football for a living means that our physical condition is very important and if we didn't take care of ourselves when it mattered our results would soon make it clear.

Israel has become one of our regular and favourite haunts. I have been there on several occasions with Brighton, Ireland and Liverpool. Every time we are due a visit I am always asked the same question about the security situation out there. We have never seen any trouble on our visits to Tel Aviv, the people are wonderful hosts, and because of the superb climate it is always a trip that we anticipate with pleasure, even if we have been beaten on our last two appearances. Israel is an amazing place and perhaps we should not be surprised that the standard of football is improving rapidly because everything else seems to happen in a hurry, too, in that country.

I am sure airline crews have mixed feelings when a football team gets on board. Remember we are fit healthy young men, and if the club has made it clear that an end of season trip is to be enjoyed it is inevitable that we will let our hair down, although during the serious business of European competition alcohol is out of the question.

Vanessa tells a nice story about when we were at Brighton. The club had arranged a short end of season break in Majorca. Vanessa, however, was booked for a summer season with the comedian Ken Goodwin at Eastbourne, so it would have been impossible for us to have a holiday if I had waited for the Brighton trip. I explained the problem to Alan Mullery and he agreed to let me take Vanessa out a week before the team and I would join up with them when she returned for the summer season.

Apparently Vanessa was on the plane which had brought the Brighton players out. There was a young child crying on board and Vanessa sympathised with the cabin crew. 'You have certainly got your hands full there' she said. The stewardess replied 'This is nothing. We have just brought out a bunch of footballers from Brighton and they drove us crazy.' 'Really' said Vanessa, refraining from saying anymore about it.

THE GOOD, THE BAD AND ...

Injuries are inevitable in football simply because it is a contact sport and you have to accept that somewhere along the line you are going to be hurt. I have had various operations during my career, yet my most serious injuries have been complete accidents and not the result of attention from some hit man. There are plenty of those around but they are not all defenders. The popular theory is that if a game is getting a bit rough, the advantage lies with defenders, because for most of the time forwards have their backs to their markers and cannot see what is coming.

I have never regarded myself as a hard case and I do not think my reputation in the game suggests it either. Of course, I put everything into a tackle and when you are committed you must expect to collect a few scars as mementoes. I learnt that lesson at an early stage scrambling about the pitch in a game against Grimsby, trying to find what was left of my four front teeth which were scattered in little bits after coming into contact with somebody's elbow. Nearly every player has lost teeth one way or another, and there is no shortage of broken noses either, but you can take the knocks as long as they come your way legitimately. Jack Charlton got into trouble with the authorities some 20 years ago for revealing that he had a little black book with the names of players he was waiting for, to avenge something that had happened in previous games. I will never get to that stage but the villains are well known by their fellow professionals and we keep a wary eye on them whenever we come into contact.

Of the present day players I suppose David Speedie is recognised as a bit of a handful, and although I have had some fierce battles with him I can honestly say we get on like a house on fire off the pitch. When you play against Speedie you know what to expect. He may be small but he is very aggressive and he likes to unsettle you as early as he can in a game. He does not belong to the sneaky brigade, however, it is all up front with Speedie and out in the open. 147

The first time I played against him I was booked and might have been sent off, it was that type of confrontation, and it is not often I get myself into hot water with referees, but with Speedie it is a battle from the start. He knows that if he kicks you he can expect to be kicked in return, and he accepts that that is the way it is. He had the last laugh in that first clash, by scoring a goal and Chelsea won the match.

Most central defenders would prefer to mark an orthodox centre forward, even if he is bigger and stronger than themselves. I am around the six foot mark but you could not call me a heavyweight, so I can be knocked around by a big man, but I prefer that type of opponent to someone like Speedie or Peter Beardsley, two of the smaller men but with sufficient strength and skill to make life difficult for a tall defender.

The best in the business without doubt is Ian Rush. I have never played against him and I am quite happy for that situation to remain unchanged. Rushie falls between the 'big 'uns' and the 'little 'uns' in a physical sense, but as a striker he is the one defenders least like to face. I have not had that experience even in training sessions because we never go in for tackling at Liverpool when we are working at Melwood.

Football is all about touch play and accuracy of passing so Rushie has not had the chance to worry me, but watching him in action for Liverpool on match days convinces me there is nobody quite like him. A defender is at an immediate disadvantage if he knows the man he is marking has the edge in pace and in Rushie's case it is usually more than just an edge. Over 10 to 20 yards he can be devastating. With the possible exceptions of Kevin Ratcliffe, Paul McGrath and maybe David O'Leary, I cannot think of any defenders who can catch him when he is in full flight. That amazing acceleration is often shown at its most effective when Rushie is taking the ball away from defenders. So many times a player may be dwelling on the ball confident he has time because there is nobody near him, when without any warning Rushie has swooped and whipped the ball away from him to set up another attack.

When it comes to scoring he has another advantage which few other strikers possess. He never needs more than one touch on the ball when he is bearing down on goal. If he collects the ball in full flight in or around the penalty area nine times out of 10 it will end up in the back of the net because he never needs to correct himself. He always makes sure he has it under control, that is what makes him an exception. If I am in trouble or trying to retrieve a difficult situation I know I have a chance if I can close down the opponent before he has the ball completely under control because the odds are he will try to steady himself before taking a shot. Rush does not do that, he has sufficient confidence in his ability to go with it first time with no question of any hesitation.

That is why I would never compare Gary Lineker with Rush. Perhaps it is because Lineker plays for England and was under the spotlight in the 1986 World Cup when he finished the top scorer that some people put him in the same bracket as Ian. But not me. Gary is very good, he also has a sprinter's finish, but his all-round game is not in Rushie's class and he does like a second touch on the ball before he aims for goal. I think Gary will get even better than he is now but so will Rushie. His peak is still to come and it is just a shame that it will be Juventus and not Liverpool who will enjoy the benefits of owning the world's number one striker. Yes, he is that good, and I have not forgotten Diego Maradona either.

I have often wondered just what Ian and Kenny Dalglish might have achieved together if they were the same age. Despite the 11 years which separate them, they were a marvellous combination for Liverpool when the boss was playing regularly. I have only faced Kenny once, when I was at Brighton, and that was an education in itself. He is not particularly big, he would never claim to be one of the quickest around even in his prime, but for sheer animal cunning he was in a class of his own. Kenny is the thinking man's footballer. He has all the ability, but it is his quickness of mind which makes him so special and a nightmare for defenders. He invites you to tackle him, daring you to commit yourself and if you fall for it and dive in he has suddenly disappeared and you are floundering on the ground wondering where the devil he's gone.

Anybody who tackles Kenny inside the penalty area is 149

also asking for trouble because he has turned penalty claims into an art form. But if you don't tackle him he is liable to score anyway so it is a *Catch 22* situation for any defender. I am told he had something of an off day when I played against him, if that is so I can only be grateful, because I saw enough in that game at Anfield to convince me he was quite different from any other forward I had come across, either in this country or abroad. I have marvelled at his skill from the comparative safety of the Liverpool penalty box.

More often than not I find myself in direct opposition to a big centre forward and I know that they are going to come at me with elbows flying, particularly for the aerial challenges. That is what centre forwards are there for and if they didn't make an impression they wouldn't be doing their job. Again the majority of the so-called hard nuts are very up front, even if it means a black eye now and again. Joe Jordan came into that category. He was quite fearless, and you expected a bit of a battering when you tangled with him, but there was never anything underhand with Joe. He set out to expose any weakness you might have, but if you dished some back he took it without any complaint.

I much prefer the Joe Jordans of the game from a personal point of view. There are plenty of big target men around today in a similar mould; Niall Quinn of Arsenal is one. He is so tall he presents an immediate problem but you are not going to be taken by surprise by him.

It is just a headache trying to get up in the air with a guy who is four or five inches taller than you. Alan Smith, also now at Arsenal is another, so is Mick Harford – they are both strong target men who will always be trying to beat you in the air. I know that is not the strongest part of my game, in fact Gary Gillespie is the most effective central defender we have for challenging big men in the air, although Alan Hansen can obviously cope with it.

Over the years Liverpool has not had a really dominating centre half who could tower over a big centre forward. Ron Yeats, now the club's chief scout, was probably the last one, but it does not seem to have done us any harm. Emlyn Hughes and Tommy Smith were both powerful players, though hardly giants, yet they were recognised as outstanding central defenders; so was Phil Thompson, now the club's reserve coach. He was so slim he made me look positively overweight.

At Liverpool defenders concentrate on playing constructively rather than merely relying on power. The important thing when you are faced with a centre forward who has a reputation for being dangerous in the air, is to contain him outside the penalty area, if possible, where he is not going to do any damage. If we're inside the box I always challenge because I know there will be some back-up if the ball runs loose.

Kevin Keegan certainly came into the Dalglish/Beardsley/Speedie bracket from a physical point of view. I always admired Kevin because I don't think he was the most naturally gifted player around but he made the most of what he had. He worked hard and gained the rewards. He also paid me one of the nicest compliments I have ever received. After we had played Newcastle in a Cup tie he said he knew it was time to call it a day when I made up five yards on him to win the ball. What he did not say was that I was probably in my prime, while he was over 30. It might have been a different story if that incident had occurred a few years earlier because Kevin was very quick and, for a small man, a considerable threat in the air. I don't think Kevin was in the same class as Dalglish as a player, good though he was, and I wouldn't compare him with Rushie when it comes to scoring goals because there would be only one winner.

Pace has always been my chief weapon against any striker and I can honestly say that I have never been really worried about facing anyone on that score. Lineker is probably the fastest man I have had to deal with. If he gains half a yard on you, the odds are always going to favour him in a one-to-one situation, but again I would put Rush ahead of him for sprinting speed and acceleration off the mark. I am not putting Lineker down, it is just that every time I compare him with Rush, Gary is the loser; compare him with someone else and it might be different. Rush has been scoring regularly at the highest level for the last six years at a rate of 30 or 40 goals a season. Perhaps he has done it in a successful team but nobody is marked more tightly because of his reputation.

If you start in the lower divisions as I did, you soon learn how to take care of yourself because they are a tough training ground, especially if you are a raw youngster coming up against somebody who has been around for a long time and has seen it all before, probably at a higher level.

Apart from losing my teeth at an early age, I collected some other scars in those days. You could call it part of my soccer education because it is in the basement that most of the fishy business takes place. The bloody noses and cuts and bruises are fair enough but you quickly learn to look out for the type of player who deliberately sets out to hurt you; what's more, the slightest lapse in concentration can cost you dear. Rachid Harkouk taught me that when he was with Crystal Palace. A tackle delivered a split second too late meant that I had to have eight stitches in my shin.

Bobby Gould, now manager at Wimbledon, was also a master of the late challenge, which he usually reserved for goalkeepers. Many an unsuspecting keeper who thought the ball was safely in his grasp was flattened by Gould coming it at top speed.

You learn, sometimes the hard way, the steps you need to take to protect yourself physically and psychologically. Opponents will always be testing you to see if you can be conned into losing your temper and, with it, your self control. Ken Beamish certainly caught me out in a Cup tie when I was with Brighton and he was playing for Tranmere. We had won the first leg comfortably at the Goldstone, but I fell for the five card trick in the return. I can honestly say he tried to tackle me just below the hip and for the next five minutes I just went crazy. Ken, an old pro who had played for a lot of clubs including Brighton, obviously set out to try and unsettle me. If that tackle did not do any physical damage it certainly wrecked my concentration and I was eventually sent off for a remark to a linesman. I was still fuming as I headed for the tunnel and looked across at Beamish who gave me a sly wink. Sure, the laugh was on me, but it was a lesson I have never forgotten.

In my first season at Liverpool I came across Kenny Burns. He had been moved into attack because Leeds were struggling at the time, and he was determined to let me know he was around. The game was only a couple of minutes old when I tackled him for the first time, and played the ball forward. The next thing I knew, I was lying on the ground with my head spinning because Kenny had laid me out! It is fair to say that I got my own back in the second half, but being a genuine hard case, Kenny took it without any complaints. No matter how aggressive they are, certain players earn the respect of their fellow pros because they can take tough tackles as well as dish them out.

It is not just defenders and strikers who have to be able to take care of themselves. A lot of the action goes on in mid-field, and the name of Johnny Giles would always crop up when the subject of mid-field generals was the topic. I saw that for myself in a European championship match against Bulgaria. I was not in the squad for the first game in Sofia but I heard all about it before the second leg in Dublin. Apparently, Johnny had kicked a magnificent 30-yard equaliser to cancel out Bulgaria's lead, only for it to be disallowed because it was offside. This clearly delighted one Bulgarian player who made his feelings quite clear on the pitch. The Irish lads were livid because nobody was interfering with play and all the coaching staff and substitutes leapt up from the touch line to demonstrate. At most grounds in the Communist bloc soldiers ring the perimeter and in Sofia they immediately moved towards the Irish lads who had no option but to sit down again. Noel Campbell was sent on soon after the goal had been disallowed and he got his marching orders within 10 minutes of joining the action. It was that sort of game.

I was in the squad for the return at Lansdowne Road. As the two teams walked out together, Johnny was studying the Bulgarian players to see if the guy who had annoyed him so much in Sofia was in the team. When Johnny spotted him he told the rest of us very quietly to leave the Bulgarian to him. For half an hour Giles didn't have a chance to get near the guy, but then it all changed. The Bulgarian got the ball on the half way line with his back to our goal and as he turned, Johnny tackled him with everything he had. The Bulgarian had to go off for treatment never to return. There were a lot of stories about Johnny but I only teamed up with him in the closing stages of his playing career. When you have been around as long as he had it is inevitable that you learn how to take care of yourself. He was hardly built to play the hard man role, yet those who knew him from past experience never took any liberties when he was on the pitch.

There is an old saying that those who live by the sword die by it and that still applies today. If you want to make a reputation for yourself as someone to be feared you must expect to face the consequences at some time in your career. There is a big difference between that and earning the respect of your fellow professionals for your ability. I know which course I prefer.

Not all big centre forwards rely on physical strength. Kerry Dixon is a case in point. He is one of the best finishers around, and dangerous in the air, but he relies on timing rather than power to get the better of you. I do not claim to know what went wrong for Kerry last season, but I am sure the nose dive in his form is only temporary because at one stage he looked like the answer to England's prayers.

One centre forward who seems to improve every season is Graeme Sharp of Everton. He has the knack of hanging in the air and wins plenty of free kicks that way when the defender is ruled to have pushed him. I know that to my cost; once you are committed to making a challenge it is inevitable that there will be physical contact. It is all part of the game and Graeme is a thinking centre forward who is always trying to get the advantage. Everton's emergence as a major force in recent years is all down to Howard Kendall – I wonder if he remembers presenting me with a medal at a school prize-giving ceremony in Preston?

THE CRICKET FACTOR

Next to soccer I have always loved cricket, and I remain a fan to this day. As a boy I was equally keen on both sports and whenever it is possible I still go to Old Trafford to watch Lancashire and I have made many good friends at the county. Jack Simmons stands out because he has a great interest in soccer, too. He was on the board of directors at Burnley for a spell and has been a friend for many years. At one stage I was offered a place on the ground staff at Lancashire but when I was forced to make the choice I had no hesitation in opting for soccer and with hind-sight I am sure I made the right decision.

My appetite was whetted as a schoolboy when we had a day out at Old Trafford to watch what is still remembered as an epic Gillette Cup game against Gloucester. My stepfather was in the players' pavilion that day as Lancashire won in the gathering dusk in an amazing finish. I can still see Mike Procter taking an enormous run up to stretch the time out for Gloucester and all the Lancashire fans howling with impatience. The Lancashire boys were the one-day kings then, with Jack Bond as captain. He is a regular visitor to Anfield because he has become a big Liverpool fan, but on that day I was mesmerised by the excitement and suspense as Lancashire clinched their victory in a nail-biting finish. David Hughes, now the county captain, hit 20-plus off one over to clinch it for Lancashire and from then on I was hooked on the game.

I played for my local club, Penwortham, and progressed to Preston Schoolboys and eventually the County Schoolboys team. I had two indoor trials for Lancashire before being invited to Old Trafford to work in the nets under the supervision of the senior coach. When the offer to join the ground staff came I was 16 and very excited at the prospect, but it was made plain to me that I would need to work very hard at my game to have any chance of making the grade and that would mean soccer taking a back seat. At the end of the day, therefore, the choice was made for me, because I was not prepared to give up soccer, so regretfully, my cricket career was destined to become no more than a very pleasant hobby.

I would love to think that I could have combined the two sports, but to be honest, I doubt whether I would have made it at cricket even though I did manage a couple of centuries as a youngster. A few years ago it was possible to play both as a full-time career. The Compton brothers, Denis and Leslie certainly made it work, and in more recent times so did Luton goalkeeper, Jim Standen, who also played county cricket. But the numbers playing both sports have dropped off because of the increasing demands of soccer. Phil Neale managed it for a number of years playing soccer for Lincoln and captaining Worcester and, Jim Cumbes, another goalkeeper with Aston Villa, was a fast bowler for Warwickshire.

Arnie Sidebottom, who played for Manchester United, actually made the Test team when he played full-time cricket for Yorkshire. Another goalkeeper, Steve Ogrizovic of Coventry, still squeezes in a few games for Shropshire and always looked a useful bowler when he was at Liverpool and played the summer game for Southport. You won't find many people who have the time to combine the two sports at professional level these days.

I have always got along with the Lancashire lads and include Frank Hayes, David Hughes and David Lloyd among my friends, and it was quite a thrill when I was introduced to the great Clive Lloyd. When I go to Old Trafford these days I am always made very welcome and it is a case of being killed with kindness if you are not careful, that is how generous they are.

The financial rewards may not be as great for cricketers but they certainly have a better social life. Cricket is considered less demanding than soccer, but the way the game has changed I am not so sure about that. They play seven days a week in a variety of competitions and I know from experience that there is nothing more tiring than being out in the field all day. Anyone who thinks that is an easy number should try it, especially if it is a hot day. It's no joke being on the receiving end when the two batsmen are hitting strongly for six hours at a stretch.

Cricket is a harder game to learn when you are a young-ster. One mistake as a batsman and you are usually out, whereas in football, unless you are a goalkeeper, you always get a second chance. The concentration required is different, too. I can remember being drained when I managed my two centuries; it was only when it was over that I realised how much the effort had taken out of me, and that was just in a local game. What goes on in the mind of a Test batsman when every move and stroke is analysed on television and radio is something else. That is why I have always been a big admirer of Geoff Boycott's. He was accused of being selfish and a slow scorer but anyone who can switch off from everything and stay at the wicket for hours on end must have a very special quality which few can hope to emulate.

I managed to carry on playing cricket at club level when I was with Brighton. There are some beautiful grounds down in Sussex and we had quite a good team. Our captain was a guy called Jim Pegg and he was a one-legged wicketkeeper – honestly. A Football League referee, Martin Bodenham, was a member of the team, too, but that did not count for much when we met in a match one season and he almost sent me off! I wondered whether I had done something on a balmy summer's day without realising it.

Cricketers also have a reputation for being more reliable than footballers when it comes to attending off-the-field engagements and this is probably a valid claim. I know that David Hughes, the Lancashire captain, went to the trouble of making one game at Kirkham near Blackpool for charity part of the official fixture list to ensure everybody turned up. It is not often you will get a full soccer team at every event, although to be fair, we certainly do our share at Liverpool. Things have changed over the years; at one time the requests would be just for autographs, then they were for autographed footballs, and today it seems nothing less than an autographed football shirt will suffice. We do try to fit in as many functions as we can but there is a limit to what we can do, which is something that people don't always understand.

SELF-STYLED PUNDITS

Football provides more talking points than any other sport simply because more people are interested in it, but am I in the minority when I despair at constantly reading in some newspapers the sniping attacks which bear the names of ex-players who have earned a damn good living out of the game?

I do not claim to be an expert on what sells newspapers and if that is the kind of thing which boosts circulation then the people in charge may have a valid point. What they do is their business, but when I see famous names from the past racing in to knock the game which has been so good to them I do ask the question whether they really need the money so badly. It is one thing to hear a debate in the pub among genuine fans who love to talk football – none more so than those on Merseyside – but it is another thing when people are getting well paid to take a swipe at the game and individuals in it simply because they have a famous name, thanks to football.

Three such personalities spring immediately to mind – John Bond, Mike Channon and Emlyn Hughes. They have all done very nicely out of football, but they seem to have developed their own cottage industry in which everyone and everything is fair game. Emlyn was an outstanding player, although not the most popular in the Anfield dressing room according to stories I have heard, and he certainly made the game pay. There is nothing wrong with that. He was a captain of Liverpool and England so the rewards were guaranteed to be good, but I shall be very surprised if he is not earning more today as a television personality and newspaper pundit.

A Question of Sport has been a big success and it is the way that Emlyn, and Billy Beaumont, as the resident chairmen, react to each other that has such an appeal to viewers. Again that is fine, Emlyn does have a good delivery on the box and I am told that the big smile is very popular with women viewers. But every time an England international game comes around Emlyn changes faces and suddenly becomes Bobby Robson's arch critic. That is what I do not understand. As a former captain of the national team why does he have to seek the headlines? Is it ego, image or just the money? I have no axe to grind with him at a personal level, although some of the tales I have heard about him from former Liverpool players would certainly confuse the viewers. They see him as a happy, bouncy character able to mix easily with all sections of the community from Royalty down.

As I recall, he was not a great success in his short stint in management so what credentials has he got for pinning Bobby Robson against the wall? These attacks invariably come when an England game is imminent and Emlyn passes judgement on the team selected and gives his opinions, usually negative, about their prospects.

Maybe it is harder these days to divide sport from entertainment. I think the BBC see Emlyn as a foil for the Saint and Greavsie show on ITV, but does he really need to be so negative? Is there a big name open-season to take a poke at anyone you choose?

England won the World Cup in 1966 and playing all their games at Wembley certainly helped. Since then very little success has come their way in terms of trophies but if you look at the results under Bobby Robson who else is better equipped to pick the team? Brian Clough has his backers, and rightly so, but apart from him and possibly Terry Venables, there are not many obvious candidates. Perhaps Emlyn thinks he should get the job, but bearing in mind his present status – as a television performer rather than a football player – I really don't see how he has the nerve to criticise Robson no matter how big the pay cheque.

I was appalled to read an article with the name of Mick Kennedy of Portsmouth on it soon after they had won promotion. He was criticising some of the biggest names in the country, Glenn Hoddle and Charlie Nicholas included, and implying that they were all in for a shock when Portsmouth kicked off their new season back in the First Division. Whoever advised him to say all that was doing the players and the game a grave disservice. I was in the Brighton team which won promotion to the First Division and the last 159 thing you do is start shouting the odds before you have met the big boys. Mr Kennedy has already made himself a few enemies with long memories before he has kicked a ball in the First Division.

It has been a long time coming but, belatedly, the PFA has sent out a directive warning all players not to make verbal attacks on rival players and managers, and to bear in mind that we are all in this game together and make a very good living from it.

We should not, therefore, be sticking knives in each other's backs. Maybe I am old fashioned but I am amazed that the Football League and the FA have not joined forces with our own Union to stop the practice. Right now we are trying to get back into Europe and our image is under constant scrutiny. Can you imagine what a UEFA official might think if he happened to be in this country and picked up a paper with Mick Kennedy's comments in it? It is the easiest thing in the world to take a poke at a big name, epecially if you are being offered money to do it, but do these guys ever think of the damage they are doing to the game? I will put Kennedy's outburst down to inexperience, but I cannot excuse John Bond and Mike Channon so easily.

Channon had a long and distinguished playing career at the highest level and, as far as I know, he is not short of a bob or two, but put him on television in a World Cup year and he thinks he has a licence to call anyone any name he can think of. When he left Portsmouth he even included some of their lads in his attacks but after Kennedy's comments I can more or less understand that.

I sometimes think that these television soccer pundits see themselves as budding Terry Wogans: say something controversial and who knows what offers will come pouring in. I have always thought that Channon was too intelligent a person to be saying all this purely for effect, but the longer it goes on the more I begin to have second thoughts.

Stan Bowles, a very sad case of a man down on his luck, gave his story to a newspaper but he didn't start calling other people names, he concentrated on his own misfortune. When Joe Fagan quit at Liverpool, I am sure he had a story to tell which would have attracted plenty of offers from the media, but he chose to remain silent. Tommy Docherty also likes to take the odd poke at people but when he does so it is different. I suspect it is always tongue in cheek and delivered with a sense of humour. I have attended several dinners when he was the speaker and know he is a naturally funny man. But it is one thing to be funny and another to be malicious.

Take John Bond. Everyone was fair game for him last season when I would have thought he needed all the hours available to keep Birmingham City out of trouble. Until he got the sack he must have been one of the longest-serving managers in the game; Bournemouth, Norwich, Manchester City, Burnley and Swansea were all under his control at some stage. Before that he had played the game at the top level with West Ham. Last season the controversial Mr Bond really excelled and, apart from the long-suffering Bobby Robson, Liverpool was his biggest target.

When Paul Walsh was sent off at Southampton for punching Kevin Bond with a hook Mike Tyson would have been proud of, to my knowledge Bond senior was hundreds of miles away. But it did not stop him from bursting into print with his version of what had happened, even though he had not been there. Paul claimed that he retaliated when Bond junior spat at him. You can take it from me that Paul would not have reacted so violently if nothing at all had happened in the first place. Paul got his marching orders because he was in the wrong and knew it and, in fairness to Kevin Bond, he didn't get involved in a slanging match. In fact, he came to Anfield the following week to play twice in the Cup replay and a League match without any moans. But his father had to stick his oar in. You can argue that this is natural when a father and son are involved, but it didn't do Kevin any favours and I would not want my father, an ex-pro, or my stepfather, a Preston director, getting involved if I were in trouble.

John Bond seems unable to resist the temptation, however. After making a fool of himself when he said that Kevin would never spit at a player – he should know what goes on in the heat of the moment – he then turned his attention to Kenny Dalglish, accusing him of being a moaner. In the two years that Kenny had been manager of Liverpool, John Bond was in charge at Swansea and

Birmingham so I don't see how their paths could have crossed. He must have been basing his claims on second-hand opinion, and that is always dangerous. What he thinks of Kenny is not the point. If, in his wisdom, he decides to criticise he should be sure of his facts and at least speak from personal experience.

Bitter newspaper articles do nothing for football but, unfortunately, the same trait appears to be creeping into cricket. Because Ian Botham is now over 30 the snipers are starting to fire bullets at him for a cheap thrill. The fact that he has been one of the greatest cricketers of all time does not seem to matter. Nobody has given the game a bigger shot in the arm than this fellow nor helped his colleagues to enhance their earnings by becoming such a crowd puller. Yet as soon as he starts bowling off a shorter run he is suddenly on the rack. He is no longer the all-rounder, just the batsman, yet if you look at the statistics, and goodness knows that is what the cricketing fraternity love above all else, Botham's record says it all.

Put it down to the British obsession for placing stars on a pedestal and then delighting in knocking them off it, but in my game the attacks are increasing and can only harm football. It is something Kevin Keegan, and more recently Bryan Robson, can vouch for. They know what it is like to be built up into super guys and then be written off just as quickly. I can see Gary Lineker having the same problem in the future and it is already happening to Peter Shilton.

I have expressed my opinion of Shilton elsewhere in this book, and can only think of a handful of keepers I would rate above him, and that does not detract from what he has achieved. He has been a model pro and still is a master of his craft, yet one possible mistake against Brazil last season and suddenly the media are saying that it is all over for Peter – that's absolute rubbish. The ultimate irony is that players are always remembered fondly when they retire yet many are not appreciated while they are still playing.

Remember Peter Osgood? He was no angel on or off the field but any mention of his name to Chelsea fans today and, I will put money on it, they will only have good things to say about him. The same is true of Charlie Cooke. When he played he was always accused of being too selfish but now he is rightly remembered as one of the cleverest forwards the modern game has seen. I wonder what they will say about me? Perhaps I shouldn't tempt fate.

This is the nearest I shall get to criticising people. Where would I be if I could not play this game? I realise what it has given me and I have no intention of losing my credibility by starting to take cheap shots at people for instant rewards.

BEST AND WORST

Scarborough's elevation to the Football League brought back unhappy memories for me. On the one occasion that I played at their ground for Preston we were on the receiving end of an FA Cup upset, losing 3–2 after being two goals up. Giant killing is part and parcel of the competition, but when it is you that is left with egg on your face, you don't appreciate the so-called magic and mystery of the competition. I am pleased that they have made it to the big time but I have no wish to return to Scarborough in a hurry. Harry Catterick was our manager and he did not want the game to start because there was snow everywhere and it was so cold that the pitch was freezing up before the kick-off. Harry tried to get the game called off but it went ahead and we paid a heavy price.

The Shay at Halifax is another one near the bottom of my list of least favourite places. Even on a reasonable day it is not the most attractive place to play football, and on a murky night when the floodlights do not shine very brightly through the gloom, it can be a miserable experience. I was on the losing side there, too, with Preston, but at least Alan Ball senior enjoyed it because he was the Halifax manager at the time.

Strangely enough the Goldstone ground has not been a happy place for me either since I left. I have never been on the winning side during my visits with Liverpool and it is only since I left that I have realised what a pronounced slope there is at one end. When I was playing there regularly I hardly noticed it.

The dreaded plastic is not for me either, especially after Liverpool's meetings with Luton last season. We took an awful lot of stick for complaining about Luton, yet at no time did the boss or anybody else suggest that they were lucky to win. In fact, Kenny stressed that the better side won on the night. But in my opinion it is false football, and the sooner those pitches disappear the better. Playing on an artificial pitch produces artificial football. To be fair to

Luton, their pitch is a big improvement on the surface at QPR, which thankfully is going to disappear at the end of this season.

I am told that the best of these surfaces is at Preston, although I have not played on it. It has certainly helped to revive the fortunes of my home town club, but I am afraid I am prejudiced against the synthetic surface, and I believe the vast majority of players in the game feel the same way, including those who have to play on it regularly. Newcastle is another place I am never really comfortable in although we did put on something of an exhibition this season when Steve Nicol scored a hat trick. No matter what the weather may be like elsewhere in the country you can be sure there will be a swirling wind on Tyneside which does not help any team to give its best.

Abroad, the East European stadiums seem to have a depressing feel to them. There is nothing wrong with the facilities but you can tell you are in a Communist country. Moscow's Olympic stadium can compete with the best when you look at the layout but it seemed a drab and colourless place to me when I played there for the Republic of Ireland. Also, for obvious reasons, the less I see of the Heysel stadium in Brussels the better.

Another ground which gets the thumbs down from me is Stamford Bridge. I am sure the games would look more exciting if they could move the pitch closer to the terraces. Perhaps it suits Chelsea because of the problems they have had with some of their supporters, but I much prefer to play with the crowd breathing down my neck, and since they built their new stand at White Hart Lane, Tottenham no longer counts as one of my favourite venues. Again, it is all to do with the atmosphere or the lack of it, and White Hart Lane has lost some in my opinion.

The places I like best are more predictable. Anfield, for example, has the best playing surface in the country. If you cannot perform on that pitch you cannot do it anywhere. They did have drainage problems a few years ago but they did a magnificent job getting it right and it is always in superb condition, regardless of the weather, and stays green right through the season. It is a pity they cannot do the same thing at Old Trafford because it is one of the most 165 spectacular grounds in the country, but the pitch has been a disaster. You can be sure that for the second half of the season there will be problems at Old Trafford which will handicap United as much as they do the opposition.

Goodison Park is another great place to play. Maybe I am lucky that it is always full when I go there for a Mersey derby but it is one of the most impressive grounds in the country with a character all of its own. I like the Dell at Southampton because it is small and compact with the crowd close to the touchline. That kind of environment does fire you up for a game and I always look forward to playing there.

Wembley of course must be on the list. What strikes me about the ground is how small it looks when it is empty but it is transformed by a full house and it has provided me with some outstanding memories, not least the Mersey Cup final. I do not think the police could believe their eyes when so many rival fans behaved impeccably away from home. That was the best atmosphere I have enjoyed for any game and it must have worked wonders for the image of Merseyside and its people. The two grounds I would dearly love to savour are the Maracana in Rio de Janeiro and the Nou Camp in Barcelona – who knows, I might get the chance one day.

SPORT AND SHOW BUSINESS

With the advent of live soccer on television, playing matches has become a seven-days-a-week activity, particularly for clubs like Liverpool who are featured regularly on television.

In my time I have played on every day of the week at some stage, which does put an extra strain on your private life. I am sure most footballers' wives or girlfriends are prepared to put up with constant disruption to their home life because it doesn't last forever and if you are fortunate to play for a successful club the rewards are considerable. I have been lucky with Vanessa, because like me she is accustomed to odd working hours and the need to travel to pursue her career. I am sure that for many people, however, it does come as a considerable shock if they have a footballer as a mate.

No Monday to Friday routine, no nine to five working hours, it is a timetable which can put stress on a relationship unless both parties can come to terms with it. Vanessa had her own successful career when we met. Apart from being a professional dancer who has worked with some of the biggest names in show business she is also a member of Equity and has appeared in various television series, like *Robin's Nest* and in a couple of BBC plays. Working unusual hours was second nature to her, so she could take it in her stride when I disappeared on a Friday to travel to wherever we were playing.

Our social life does suffer, however. When live soccer was introduced on television most players preferred to play on a Friday night because it enabled them still to enjoy the traditional Saturday night out. Now Sunday has become the regular day, because television viewing figures are highest then, so the whole weekend is taken up if my team is involved. We have to train on a Saturday morning and have an early night in readiness for the game, which means that our wives and girlfriends suffer because the one night of the week when they knew they could plan something – 167

Saturday – has become just another day in a footballer's week.

Believe it or not there is another handicap to playing on a Sunday – there is nothing to occupy your mind on the morning of the match. On the Saturday there will be pop programmes and the two soccer previews but on a Sunday, unless you are interested in teaching yourself Hindi, Chinese or whatever, there is precious little to help you to while away the hours before the kick-off. I am not looking for sympathy and I don't expect to get any. I play football because I enjoy it and I get well paid to play it. But I do sometimes wonder if people with a regular working week realise how much and how often we have to change our routine. I know the majority will say they would change places tomorrow if they had the opportunity and I understand that. Football has been good to me but perhaps I realise the stresses and strains it can impose on a relationship because of my own broken marriage.

We are all liable to variable moods and I can be riding high one week, when everything is going well, and in the depths of depression only days later. There is nothing worse for a footballer than to be injured and it takes a very understanding type of person to endure the short temper of an injured athlete when he is denied the chance to do his work. That is when I need some space in my private life and Vanessa understands me well enough not to intrude on those occasions. No matter how hard I try it is impossible not to snap when I'm injured and Vanessa has told me that she sometimes hesitates to show her face if she knows I am depressed and moping about. Again those situations are even worse when you have children and it is a very demanding task keeping the household happy when there is a moody footballer nursing an injury.

I have met many big names from show business through Vanessa. Freddie Starr, Tom O'Connor, Michael Barrymore, Roy Hudd, Little and Large, Cilla Black, Les Dawson, Russ Abbott, Dana, plus the Liverpool fans, Jimmy Tarbuck and Stan Boardman. Whenever I see Freddie on the box I always remember that famous headline in the *Sun* 'Freddie Starr Ate My Hampster'. It must have been invaluable publicity for him. Tarby usually makes it to our games in the South because he lives near London and he is granted the rare favour of coming into our dressing room before a game when he can be relied on to crack a few gags and get us in a good frame of mind. Stan Boardman, a close friend of Craig Johnston's, always gives us a plug on the telly and claims to have been on the staff at Anfield before he went into show business.

Vanessa is used to the demands of show business which helps when I am invited to sporting events or to make personal appearances because she knows that once we arrive she will be largely ignored because people want to talk football and get autographs and the wife or girlfriend has no option but to take a back seat for the evening. I think it takes a special kind of woman to put up with a footballer's life and I am sure the same applies to other sportsmen and entertainers who are in the public eye. That is why Vanessa's upbringing has helped her to come to terms with me.

Vanessa went to the Italia Conti Stage School in London for three years and started appearing on the stage all over the country from the age of 18. When I first met her she was on tour with Sacha Distel so she knows what living out of a suitcase is all about and can accept it as normal. I am sure the fact that we both have careers which involve travelling makes us more tolerant of each other. In the early days I was the one stuck at home while Vanessa was away so I can understand how many footballers' wives must feel.

Meeting celebrities from other walks of life does give me a kick and I have met quite a few, but if Vanessa has introduced me to well-known figures from her business she has also met many of the people I have bumped into during my career.

I have already talked about my love of cricket, but golf is another passion of mine. Living in Southport means we often see the really big names in golf because major tournaments, including the Open, are staged in the area. There must be half a dozen championship courses all within easy reach and I have had the pleasure of meeting many of the game's top exponents. That gives me as much of a thrill as any youngster would have meeting his soccer idol for the first time. One of my biggest wishes is to meet Seve Ballesteros 169 because he is number one in my book. But I have not done too badly in the meantime. Nick Faldo, Sam Torrance, Sandy Lyle, Bernhard Langer, Paul Way have all crossed my path. Returning home with Liverpool from Holland after a pre-season tour we met a bunch of the boys who had been playing in the Dutch Open, including Des Smyth, John O'Leary and Christy O'Connor junior. A golfer on the European circuit, Chris Moody, stayed with me once and through him I met the great Jack Nicklaus, which it had always been one of my ambitions to do.

I suppose another claim to fame is that I played snooker against Steve Davis although it backfired really. During Phil Neal's testimonial year matches were arranged between some of the Liverpool players and Steve at Preston's Guild Hall. We were all given a 21–point start against Steve and any point we gained after that was worth a pound to Phil's testimonial. Put it down to the pure professional in Steve Davis but he was determined to win all the games by as wide a margin as possible even though that defeated the purpose of the exercise. Really we should have had a 60 or 70 point start because obviously none of us were going to be able to provide any real competition for the World Champion. I think I managed half a dozen shots in our game as he rattled off a century break to wipe the floor with me and also cost Phil a few bob. He is the number one and I guess it is that type of dedication in what was an exhibition game that makes him the great player he is. Dennis Taylor and Alex Higgins are two other snooker players I have met over the years.

The one sportsman that got away in my list of heroes was Bjorn Borg. I played a lot of tennis a few years ago, and when I was on holiday in Marbella the great Swede was prepared to play anyone who came along providing they would pay £400 for the experience. I know it sounds like a lot of money but part of the deal was that Borg would play to your standard for 60 minutes to ensure it was a good game. I turned up especially early one morning prepared to pay for the privilege but even at that time of the day there was a massive queue and it was impossible for me to take the chance. It is something I have regretted ever since because I would willingly have paid just for the experience of sharing the same court. So you see, even footballers have stars in their eyes when they look at sportsmen in other fields who have made it to the top.

To come back to football, Peter Beardsley and John Barnes are both in for a shock when they attend their first fancy dress Christmas party. Over the years a tradition has been established where the most expensive signing is expected to top the bill by singing a song of his choice before the assembled ranks. This meant that the doubtful privilege fell to me in my first year. I do not know how they rate as performers off the field but there will be no dodging the issue. Come to think of it, I don't know how Peter will react to all of us because we hear he is teetotal and the Christmas party is something of a special event. It is harrowing the first time so I hope Peter will choose an easy song so that everyone will join in and spare his blushes. Our new record buy will have to perform because Bruce Grobbelaar is the master of ceremonies and insists that everything is done in the correct order. In the unlikely event of any player joining Liverpool on a free transfer he must open the show and then we go right through the ranks.

The coaching staff accept that there will be some sorry figures the following morning, but it is the only time during the season when we are permitted to make fools of ourselves. It is also the day when absolutely nobody turns up late for training because we know that Ronnie Moran and Roy Evans will be looking at us very carefully, ready to make any hungover individual really suffer. Jim Beglin can vouch for that after his first Christmas party.

Training, which is always cut to around 40 minutes for humanitarian reasons, had only been going a short time when it became too much for Jim, and the overindulgence of the previous night was deposited on the grass. At least looking at Jim made the rest of us feel relatively well! There is no respite when that kind of thing happens. A constant barrage of 'How about a fried egg and bacon sandwich, Jim?' or 'I have got a stale pork pie in my pocket', is thrown at the sufferer by his sympathetic fellow players.

Ronnie Moran always says that if anybody is sick in training – and it doesn't happen very often – it is a bonus point. What he means is that at least the training is improv- 171 ing your physical condition even if it is in an extreme way. The post-party training session is a very tough one, even though it lasts such a short time, because we all know we need to sweat the excess of alcohol out and get back to normal.

One year when David Fairclough was still with us it became a big joke. Bear in mind that we were a bunch of footballers not feeling on top of the world. We were all anxious to prove to the training staff that we could take it in our stride. On that particular day it had been snowing and as it was not ideal for running it was decided that we would play some five-a-side games just to get the booze out of our blood streams. The team I was in was awarded a penalty and I took it. Davie was on the opposite side and was standing behind one of the makeshift goalposts. As soon as I struck the ball I knew it was going to hit the post. Davie was not watching but as the ball zoomed in on him somebody shouted a warning and he turned his head just as the ball hit the post and it smacked him straight in the face. It caught him right on the nose and there was blood everywhere but everybody, including Davie, saw the funny side of it because he was not seriously hurt even though his face looked a mess for a while.

The Christmas party did cause a problem one year and I bet the Birmingham City players are still wondering why we behaved so strangely after a match at Anfield. We had drawn them away in a League Cup tie and because of bad weather, we found to our horror that any replay would be postponed to the date of our annual bash. This was serious, as the hotel had been booked, the fancy dress gear hired for the night, and we knew anything but a positive result in the first game would have serious consequences. We scored first and things were looking good, but later on Birmingham equalised.

I am sure Joe Fagan, who was the manager then, thought our downcast expressions reflected our disappointment at Birmingham's goal. This was true up to a point, but what he didn't know was that all the lads were thinking that this would be the end of the Christmas party. The game finished in a draw and we trooped off wondering if our little event would have to be cancelled.

We decided that the show must go on, which if anything gave us an even greater incentive to see off Birmingham in double quick time in the replay. Unknown to Joe, we brought all our fancy dress gear to the hotel on the afternoon of the game, and laid our plans for an early departure from Anfield. It is a good job we won the replay 3–0 otherwise the party would have been a flop and Joe might well have put his foot down if he had known what was going on. As soon as the final whistle went every member of the team raced for the tunnel, much to the amazement of the Birmingham lads. The usual routine at the end of a game is handshakes all round and then a leisurely walk back to the dressing rooms, but not this night. We were like sprinters going off the blocks, and the Birmingham players were further mystified when they went into the lounge for the after-match beer to find none of us around. We had showered and changed in no time and had packed our bags for an immediate departure to the scene of the party.

That year a Cleveland comedian called Roy 'Chubby' Brown was our guest performer. Word had travelled down from Craig Johnston, Graeme Souness and David Hodgson about this distinctly blue but very funny fellow, who was something of a legend in his own part of the country but hardly known elsewhere. The lads had played us tapes of some of his concerts so we knew what to expect and he certainly fitted the bill. He was an absolute sensation, and word must have got round because in no time Chubby Brown was being booked all over Merseyside and now he is in great demand nation wide. He has appeared a few times in Southport since then, when we always try to catch his act. We like to think it was his spot at our private bash which helped to launch him to a wider audience.

THE ROAD TO STALAG LILLESHALL

I spent last summer recovering from one of the worst injuries that can happen to a professional footballer – a ruptured Achilles' tendon. It happened against Wimbledon and nobody else was involved. I knew it was a bad injury and when I read the newspapers later on which were linking Liverpool with several central defenders I began to wonder if they knew something I was not aware of. But I have been assured by the medical people that I can make a complete recovery and resume my career and that is all that mattered to me during the summer weeks when I was immobilised.

Injuries are something you must live with. When Ian Rush started his last season for Liverpool he said he intended to play every game and he did. He was our only ever-present player but he knows he needed a slice of good fortune for that to happen. It was still quite an achievement because there were a few guys around who would have been only too pleased to make the cheap claim that they had stopped him from playing. Considering he operated in the most vulnerable position of all and knew he was leaving at the end of the season, his dedication to our cause was the complete answer to any would-be critics who thought his heart would no longer be in the job.

Rushie has the same philosophy as I have. You cannot afford to think about being injured when you go out to play because if you do, and hold back, the odds are that it will happen. Just as I believe that results are in the lap of the gods, I think the same applies to injuries; you must risk being hurt if that is your job, and if you have the misfortune to get injured, well, so be it.

There are more important things in life than football, believe it or not, even when it is your living. At the end of the day, health is everything; you cannot put a price on that no matter how rich or famous you may become. If anything happens to us at Liverpool we all know how well taken care of we will be. Bob Paisley is a qualified physiotherapist and now we have Paul Chadwick to look after us in that department. He is a very experienced physiotherapist with his own practice, apart from his interest in Liverpool Football club. Physios are becoming increasingly important for football clubs because there does seem to have been an increase in injuries over the years, and it is essential to have someone who can get to the root of the problem quickly. The PFA have made a point of this, too, trying to ensure that every club has a qualified physiotherapist, and it was put on the agenda at the School of Excellence at Lilleshall recently.

The same applies if surgery is required. When my shoulder was dislocated in Dublin I stayed overnight before flying back the next day. There was a message at the airport telling me to report to Fazackerley Hospital right away. Vanessa picked me up and when we arrived at the hospital we were met by Roy Evans and ushered upstairs to an anteroom near the operating theatre. We were issued with hospital gowns and over-shoes and put in a room to await the surgeon, Richard Calver. When he arrived he was covered in blood because he had come straight from a hip operation. He still found time to fit me with the latest sling designed to reduce my discomfort to a minimum and told me exactly what I could do at that stage before he returned to the theatre.

It just shows that there are degrees of value. If we are tempted to imagine that we are important because we are football stars we should stop and think about the people who perform vital operations every day. In the same way that schoolboys look up to us, professional athletes appreciate the work that surgeons do. These are the people who make it possible for us to continue in our chosen profession through their skill and knowledge. I know that the operation on my shoulder was performed to the highest standard because Mr Calver passed his examination for that particular surgical procedure as a result. I was certainly more than happy to be his guinea-pig on that occasion.

Many players have their careers cut short because of illness or injury and the number of ex-Preston players who come into this category is surprisingly high. The saddest example of all was Mel Holden, a big centre forward from Scotland who might easily have made it right to the top; I know Preston thought he had the potential. At 6 ft 3 in he 175 was good in the air and the perfect target man. He soon started attracting attention from the bigger clubs and eventually moved to Sunderland, but when that did not work out he tried his luck in Holland before returning to this country with Blackpool.

Bob Stokoe was in charge at Bloomfield Road and it did not take him long to write off Mel, criticising him in the press saying that he could not run or control a ball properly. Bob was not to know at the time, and nor was anyone else, that Mel was ill and trying to battle on in a profession where anything less than complete physical fitness soon lets you down. Eventually multiple sclerosis was diagnosed which not only signalled the end of Mel's playing career but eventually cost him his life. Clearly, Mel had been suffering from the disease at the time of Bob's outburst and I am sure that the manager was as shattered as anyone when the truth was discovered, although he was only trying to produce a response from Mel when he'd ticked him off. Every manager does this when he is not satisfied with a player's perform-ance. Mel was at Preston when I was starting out and I remember him as a really likeable lad, always ready with a wisecrack and very popular with his team-mates. Because of his condition he was eventually confined to a wheel-chair before his untimely death. Fortunately, such tragedies do not occur very often, but Preston players seem to have suffered more than most.

Mike Elwiss can reflect on that because although his career ended prematurely, it was through injury rather than serious illness. He seemed destined for big things when Bobby Charlton signed him from Doncaster. He was a centre forward with a good scoring record and he formed a lethal partnership with Alex Bruce. He played in two Cup ties against Liverpool when he was with Doncaster and nearly moved to Anfield. Geoff Twentyman, who was the chief scout at Liverpool in those days and played a major role in bringing Ian Rush to the club, told me that he considered Mike to be the best striker outside the First Division. Instead of going to Liverpool Mike finished up at Crystal Palace where his career came to a premature end because of a knee injury. He had several operations to try to over-come it without success, before returning to Deepdale where he tried in vain to resurrect his career. Now he runs a Leisure Centre in Preston and his father-in-law is on the board at North End.

My closest pal at Preston was Gary Williams, and his career ended at an early stage, too. He followed me from Deepdale to Brighton before joining Crystal Palace where he managed only a few games before a knee injury finished him. At Brighton he hardly missed a game but he was so slim that his body was not built to sustain the serious knock which he received at Palace. Brighton gave him a testimonial and he has stayed in the town running a television and video shop.

Mick Baxter was another player hit by the Preston jinx. When I made the reserve team, Mick and his brother Stuart were the first team centre backs. Mick looked a very good player, a tall commanding type who seemed destined to make his mark. He was eventually signed by Middlesbrough for £300,000 and everything looked rosy for him. I do not know what happened there, but his career seemed to stand still in the North East and instead of progressing further up the ladder Mick appeared to be marking time. In the end he left for Portsmouth on a free transfer and I thought at the time it was just the break he needed because there was no question about his ability.

Then I heard that he had contracted a form of cancer and required radiation treatment to combat it. He lost his hair and a lot of weight and there was considerable concern about him. Mick is back at Deepdale now happily able to earn his living arranging for local teams from the community to use the plastic pitch and he also manages to do some coaching with the youngsters. He cannot speak too highly of Portsmouth. It seems they did everything in their power to look after him, even though he was never able to play a game for them.

In a game which is too often regarded as greedy and concerned only with itself, it is gratifying to know that there are still people around who can think beyond the result on Saturday. I know Mick will not forget the kindness and support he received from the people at Fratton Park.

The worst injury of my career introduced me to one of the most remarkable characters it has been my pleasure to

177

meet – Graham Smith, the man in charge of the magnificent National Rehabilitation Centre located at Lilleshall. I owe him and his superb back-up team an enormous debt of gratitude for putting me back on the right road after one of the most serious injuries any footballer can experience.

It happened in March 1987 in a League match against Wimbledon at Anfield when I ruptured my Achilles' tendon and was effectively put out of action for six months. Thanks to Graham, I believe I am as good as new again and the work he is doing with injured sportsmen and sportswomen is becoming known nation wide. The centre has not been in existence very long, but more and more people who earn their living in sport will start to use his facilities. Word is spreading like wild fire that if you have a problem, Lilleshall is the place to go.

Little did I know what was in store when I sustained my injury because it seemed nothing at all at the time. I am still not sure how it happened beyond the fact that it was a total accident and I suspect the chances of it happening again are a million to one. There was nobody near me as I went for the ball and the next thing I knew I had collapsed in a heap on the pitch. The nearest player to me was John Fashanu and my immediate thought was that he must have clipped me at the back of my foot. As there was no reaction from the crowd, however, I am sure that this was not so and the referee George Courtney waved play on.

I was lying on the ground, not feeling any pain and wondering what on earth had happened. I tried to get up but there was no feeling in my leg or foot. I thought I had trapped a nerve so I tried to knock my foot against the ground but I could still not feel a thing. Although my foot was flat on the pitch it felt as though it was on a slope. I turned to the referee and shouted 'I can't feel anything in my foot and you will have to get the trainer on'. Ronnie Moran and Roy Evans duly appeared and I told them I could not support myself on the leg so they had no option but to carry me off.

Back in the dressing room they removed my boot and sock but there was nothing to see. I still couldn't feel anything so they put some ice against my foot to see if that would bring any sensation back, while the club physiotherapist

Paul Chadwick was making his way down from the stand. When he examined me on the treatment table he couldn't find anything either so he made me stand up with my back to him. That was when he spotted it. There wasn't a gaping hole in the back of my leg, but there was a dent where my Achilles' tendon used to be, just above the ankle. I wasn't in any pain even though I was in a mild state of shock at the news. I was able to have a bath, get changed and hop down to the players' lounge. The game was still going on when Paul drove me to the casualty ward at the hospital where the doctor confirmed Paul's diagnosis.

It is often the case, I find, that when you need the man you know and trust, he is rarely available. When Kevin MacDonald broke his leg at Southampton it was impossible for Richard Calver, the man who looks after the Liverpool players, to tend him. When Jim Beglin suffered a similar fate in a Mersey derby Mr Calver happened to be away. In my case he was on holiday when the Wimbledon game was played. This may sound as though Mr Calver is never there when he is wanted, but it is pure coincidence that when three of us sustained serious injuries at the club he was not around. Nine times out of 10 he is on call but those are usually the occasions when he is not required. I was lucky because the man who came to my aid was a specialist in tendon injuries. His name was Mr Ghorbal and he knew exactly what my problem was before he had taken his jacket off. He just put his hand to the back of my leg and confirmed that my Achilles' tendon was torn.

The operation was arranged for the same evening but the hospital was full and it looked as though I would have to go into one of the big wards. To be honest I didn't fancy that because I didn't want to become the centre of attention just because I was an injured footballer. An unnamed Liverpool supporter has my gratitude for volunteering to give up his side room so I could be admitted without any fuss or commotion.

I was due for the operation at 8 pm and went through the usual ritual which always precedes a trip to the theatre. It seemed strange to be in hospital waiting for an operation when I felt no discomfort or pain. At 7.30 pm there was a knock on the door and I thought 'Here we go, it's my turn

179

now' but it was a nurse to tell me that someone had been brought in with a ruptured spleen and that he would have to go before me. It was around 10 pm when I went in and the next morning when I awoke, Mr Ghorbal assured me that the operation had been a success, but it was still a big shock to find my leg completely immobilised in a full-length plaster. I thought that only the area around my ankle would be in plaster but Mr Ghorbal told me that I would be stuck with the contraption for two and a half weeks. To soften the blow he added that there was no reason why I should not be able to resume my career, which put my mind at rest.

When the plaster came off I was able to start stretching exercises as the long road to regaining full fitness opened up before me. It was obvious that our club physiotherapist could spend only a limited amount of time with me because he has other commitments besides working with Liverpool players. That's where Lilleshall came in. Less than a year before my accident, the National Rehabilitation Centre had been installed to go with the Soccer School of Excellence for outstanding young footballers.

Steve Nicol had been the first Liverpool player to sample their treatment to help him recover from a hernia operation. In a way, he was the club's guinea-pig, but apart from warning me that the work was very tough and demanding, he didn't really give me much idea of what to expect. I think Liverpool was impressed by Steve's physical condition when he returned to Anfield, and he certainly started the season in tremendous form, scoring goals from full back and mid-field and getting an immediate recall into the Scottish squad. The director of the centre is an amazing man called Graham Smith, who was in the RAF in Germany, before returning to this country to mastermind the set-up.

My first impression of the place was that the people in charge meant business, and that this was going to be no gentle introduction to the art of regaining fitness. They did a great job on me in the three weeks I spent with them. Even though I missed all the pre-season training at Anfield I believe the work I did at Lilleshall was just as demanding and Graham and his team helped me to regain total physical fitness. Many other footballers have sampled their vigorous
schedules and have reason to thank them. Everything

needed to bring you up to scratch is available – a big gym, playing pitches, cycling and running routes, Graham's own personal torture chamber, treatment tables with the latest machines – it's all there, except for the swimming pool.

To give you an idea of how arduous the schedule can be, let me run through a typical week. To begin with, you need a letter of introduction from your club or specialist detailing what operation you have undergone and what stage of recovery you have reached. The first person you see at Lilleshall is the resident doctor in order to double check that you are ready for what is to follow. Then you meet the staff. Apart from Graham and his assistant, Phil Newton, there are two other full-time physiotherapists. In my first week, there were no more than a dozen footballers attending, so the ratio of one physiotherapist to every three players guaranteed constant supervision and first-class treatment.

You couldn't hope for the same degree of attention at your club because most have only one physiotherapist on call and he could be looking after half a dozen players at the same time, with the first priority being to ensure their fitness for the next game. At Lilleshall that was not the case. We started work every morning at 9 am and did not finish until 5 pm. On my first day I reported in at lunch time and started work at 2 pm. I was taken onto one of the pitches by a physiotherapist for running exercises for just over an hour. No problem, but that opening session was designed to gauge my level of fitness and how far I had progressed in training at my club. The guy who took me out was called Craig but he was soon renamed Klaus because of his Teutonic discipline and his unflinching efforts to extract the maximum out of me.

Craig had his own special plot of land at Lilleshall where we all suffered in the name of fitness. This torture stretch measured approximately 100 yards in length with an eight foot slope situated away from the football pitches. The grass is allowed to grow long on Craig's little plot and regularly watered. I had to run up it, down it, across it, around it, in every possible direction, and my legs told me how much they were suffering. At the end of Craig's session there was a short break for a cup of tea followed by a series of games with a difference.

181

I would call them the sit-down Olympics. Some of the guys were still on crutches, or in plaster, or hobbling on sticks, but when you sit down you are all equal and you would be surprised how many games Graham could devise to be played sitting down. Ever tried sit-down cricket? Or sit-down volley ball? I can assure you they are both possible because I have played them. Those games brought the spirit of competition to everybody regardless of their injuries and put everybody on the same level. All the games were treated seriously and the refereeing was harsh. There were automatic penalties for swearing or for trying to bend the rules and I soon realised that it was not wise to do either unless I wanted lots of extra press-ups to atone for my sins. There were punishments for everything and, although I never did National Service, I imagine Graham ran his centre on similar lines to the army.

Mondays would finish with a bicycle ride over a distance of four miles. Around Lilleshall there are hundreds of acres of land with farms dotted about which supply the kitchens with fresh food. The bike ride would take us past some of these establishments until we reached the main gates again. From that point it is two and a half miles back to the centre and most of it seemed to be uphill.

On Tuesday we had to be ready by 9 am to take the minibus to Newport to start the swimming exercises. There is no pool at Lilleshall yet, but they are planning to build one. At Newport, the non-swimmers are obliged to tell Graham, not that it makes much difference, because he believes everyone can swim to a certain extent. Nobody escaped scot-free even if they were forced to hang on to the side with one hand just for self-preservation. Those who were comfortable in the water started off with four lengths of the pool, just as a warm up, followed by a variety of exercises using the width of the pool. Some were designed to test weak legs, in others we would swim without using our legs at all, and in others we would do two widths under the water. We were competing against each other and the last two men in each race were ordered out of the pool to do an extra 25 press-ups. I was discovering muscles I didn't even know I had by the time Graham had finished with me.

For the races across the pool we were split up into four

teams, and the supervisor made sure that the balance was right by pairing off the weaker swimmers with at least one good performer. This was probably the most gruelling exercise of all because although we were only swimming widths, we had to get out of the pool after completing each one and dive back in when it was our turn again. We would have up to a dozen of these races at a time and, coupled with the actual swimming, it really taxed our energy. The time by now was no more than 9.45 am and to be working so hard at that stage of the morning is quite a shock for most footballers. Some of them would be just climbing out of bed if they were at home.

Before we left the swimming baths we had to endure Graham's speciality. He had two rubber bricks which were extremely heavy and he would line us up at the deep end and give us each a number. When your number was called the bricks would be dropped into the water and we had to dive down to the bottom and retrieve them within a certain time. If you didn't manage a clean pick-up at the first attempt you could forget it, because you were competing against the clock and not everybody could dive to the bottom of the pool anyway.

To finish the water sports, we played a game of polo. The good swimmers went to the deep end where they had to tread water while the lucky ones who were not so proficient had the benefit of using the shallow end where they could stand up. Then it was back to the bus for the return to Lilleshall, but those who were fit enough to run were deposited at the gates and told to make their own way back.

So by 10.30 am on a Tuesday morning we had already swum hundreds of yards and run a couple of miles and there was a lot more to come before the day was over. After a tea break we went into the gym to do exercises designed to strengthen our stomach muscles, legs and upper body. In the afternoon we went back to the pitches for more running and to step up the work we had done the previous day. If it sounds hectic it was, but the thinking at Lilleshall is that you do most of the strenuous work in the first three days and gradually slow down on Thursday and Friday. The running exercises were carefully planned to strengthen our legs. Footballers don't like working without a ball so we always had one and competed against each other in one-to-one situations just to give the running an end product.

By 4 pm it was time for another game with the inevitable penalties if we lost. If the game was sit-down cricket there would be two innings for each side and the losing team would be required to do five press-ups for each run which separated the teams at the finish. Imagine what it would entail if you had lost by an innings and a bucketful of runs! It happened on one occasion, but fortunately, I was on the winning side. The other poor blighters faced something like 240 press-ups which Graham thought was great fun.

To finish off the day it was back on the bikes again for a trip called the Lilleshall Village run – another four and a half miles with absolutely no short cuts. I don't know how Graham managed it, but all the routes seemed to be uphill. Maybe it was an optical illusion or my imagination, but I swear we always seemed to be climbing. What hurt the most was that the last mile was through a golf course and we would see players teeing off for a pleasant evening in the summer sunshine while we were slogging our guts out because we were being timed. I am sure that was all part of Graham's strategy because everything we did was planned down to the last detail.

There was no running on Wednesday mornings because Graham had a special treat for us. When we returned from the pool at Newport at 10.15 am there was a tea break and we were given time off until 11 am. That sounded nice but by then we were getting wise to him and realised there must be something coming up after such a welcome and unexpected breather. Sure enough, the treat was a six-and-a-half-mile run. I never completed it because of a stomach upset which I blame on the food at Lilleshall, but more of that later. My attempt at the distance took me all of 600 yards before I was forced to call a halt and nip into the nearest hedgerow to take emergency action. Instead of completing the course I walked back to the starting line where an astonished Graham congratulated me on setting a new lap record until he discovered just how far I had run. Running with the runs is no fun.

Dean Emerson from Coventry set the record by averaging just over six minutes a mile which is some going, especially as most of the course is uphill. Dean had been at Lilleshall for several weeks before I arrived and was obviously feeling the benefits. He missed out on Coventry's FA Cup success after suffering a knee injury before the semi finals and faced a long slog to regain fitness but Lilleshall certainly did the trick.

Wednesday afternoon belonged to Klaus – sorry Craig – and his infamous bank of land. He laid out 14 cones, seven at the top and seven at the bottom, but all in zig-zag formation. We had to run to the first cone and then back to the starting point, instead of to cone two, and then repeat the exercise until we had covered all 14 cones. This meant that we had to run up and down Craig's blasted hill covered in mud, and forcing our tired legs through the long grass until 98 cones had been accounted for. So ended the toughest part of the week; it was relatively gentle after that.

First, however, there was Graham's idea of a little light relief – a 13-mile bike ride twice round the running course with a time limit of 60 minutes. If you failed you were liable to more penalty points and more punishment. On the first lap we all put a lot into it thinking that if we were ahead of the clock we would be able to take it a little easier the second time around, but there was Graham with a stopwatch in his hand recording a time of 29 minutes at the half-way stage, so there was no respite. We might have known that Graham would have calculated just how much effort was required to complete the course in an hour. At the finish it was a close run thing for everybody involved but we just made it.

Thursday began with swimming and by this time I would not have been surprised if I had started sprouting webbed feet. I swim regularly at Southport but never under such intense pressure. At the end we had to run from the gates at Lilleshall back to the centre again. By now we were doing more ball work, much to the relief of all the footballers who were back to what they do best. After lunch there was more running and a bike ride to round off a comparatively comfortable day.

On Friday morning we did a series of exercises, 17 in all and, if we were caught malingering, the penalty was to go back to the first exercise and start all over again. The lads on crutches were also expected to do these exercises, even if it meant hopping on their one good leg to spare their damaged one. Then, those who were mobile enough went on a mile-and-a-half run to be completed in 12 minutes which may not seem too tough but after all the work that had been put in during the week it took some doing. The penalty for not completing the run in the required time was to do it all over again. By midday Friday, it was all over and we were allowed to pack our bags and go home if we had the energy to do so.

It was an experience I will not forget but I hope I don't have to go back again because that would mean there was still something wrong with my leg. I can't speak for other clubs, but we have never been expected to work so hard at Liverpool as we did at Lilleshall, even in pre-season training. I am not complaining, however, just the opposite in fact, because I know it did me the world of good. Kevin MacDonald, Jim Beglin and Jan Molby have all followed me to Lilleshall to improve their fitness after long lay-offs.

It took me three weeks of working at Lilleshall to get a clean bill of health and to start playing matches in the A-team and reserves. It might have taken me longer without the expert guidance of Graham Smith and his team. The spirit of competition they encourage for every exercise and event was important. There was a yellow tee-shirt for the worst performance, and the victim was forced to wear it for the rest of the day so that everybody would know who was the weakest person. The process was very democratic; we each had a vote and there was plenty of canvassing going on but I managed to avoid the indignity of wearing the shirt.

Lilleshall teaches you that there is always somebody worse off than yourself. Bringing together injured footballers from various parts of the country helps you to stop feeling sorry for yourself or worrying about your own progress. Ian Moores, the former Stoke and Spurs centre forward who has been playing in Cyprus, paid for his own course to get fit after trouble with his Achilles' tendon. He flew back to Lilleshall because he knew the money would be well spent. Most of us were more fortunate because our clubs payed the bills.

Brian Laws of Middlesbrough was there and he had an

interesting story to tell. He didn't know that he had a problem until he stepped up to take a penalty kick, made a complete hash of it, and collapsed on the penalty spot. At first his team-mates thought he did it because he had missed the penalty but, in fact, his knee had given way and he could not move. He had spent months rather than weeks at Lilleshall when I got there. No wonder he was one of the top performers in the bike races, but I think he will avoid taking any more penalties in the future.

Brian Kilcline, the Coventry captain who was injured in the Cup final, was also at Lilleshall and it clearly did him a power of good because he was ready to rejoin his team by the start of the season. Several Wimbledon players, including Wally Downes, Vince Jones and Andy Clement were there, as were Brendan Ormsby, Bobby McDonald and John Stiles from Leeds. Paul Hilton of West Ham, Graham Rix from Arsenal and my old pal David Langan from Oxford were also undergoing treatment. On my last week there were 25 footballers on the course, so the next time you wonder why somebody is missing from your favourite team through injury, the odds are they will be at Lilleshall. Kevin Langley arrived just 10 days after a cartilage operation, something which would have been out of the question not long ago. Lilleshall is not just reserved for footballers either. There were jockeys, a lacrosse player and a Sussex cricketer there during my time.

If I had any complaints about the place, it would be about the food, but I am a very awkward customer to satisfy. Breakfast was at 8.15 am and we had to queue for a self-service meal. Nothing wrong with that, except that I eat very little in the morning and my experience of the six mile run confirmed that the food was not agreeing with me. The accommodation is not exactly in the five star class either but I accept that you do not go there for a holiday.

The accommodation is rather basic, perhaps designed not to encourage you to hang around in your room. Each player had his own room with a bed, a sink, wardrobe, chair and table and that was about it. If you wanted a radio or a television it was up to you to provide it.

Apart from breakfast, I don't think I had more than two meals at Lilleshall during my three weeks there; my regular 187 eating place became a pub called the Fox and Duck. Most of the footballers ended up in the pub in the evening, not for the beer, but to get a good meal. There were no restrictions at Lilleshall, we could stay out as long as we wanted, but we all realised that if we went over the top it would soon become evident the next morning when Graham put us to work again. So we behaved sensibly and never forgot that we were there to regain our physical fitness and you don't do that by drinking pints.

Lilleshall was a real eye-opener for me thanks to Graham and his staff. As you get fitter you become more impatient to get back to what you do best – playing football – but when you have been out of the team for a long time at a club like Liverpool, getting back into the side can be difficult.

What you soon discover at Liverpool is that nobody is indispensable. The team can be going well with you in it when an injury forces you out for two or three weeks and your next problem is getting back, because more often than not, the team will carry on winning without you. When you have a recognised squad of 18 players who are fit and available it is obvious that you are going to have half a dozen men on the side lines every week. It is no fault of theirs, but it can be very frustrating. They often say that although nobody is ever fined or suspended at Liverpool the biggest punishment is not getting into the team.

I am hoping the fact that I can play in a variety of positions will be to my advantage while the other long-term casualties are all specialists in one role. Jan Molby and Kevin MacDonald are mid-field players and Jim Beglin is a full back. They will have noticed, just as I have, how well the team has done without us. From my point of view I want to carry on playing for Liverpool for as long as possible. Before I sustained this injury I felt I was as fit as I have been at any time in my career and although I reached my 30th birthday last summer I feel there are still a few years left in me yet. My present contract with the club has another three years to run and I do not see why I cannot complete it and possibly carry on after that. Barring injuries, and nobody can legislate against them, I am sure I can continue until I am 35. Football has been fun so far, despite the occasional setback, and I hope there are plenty more good times to come.

INDEX